OUR NEW RELIGION

JONATHAN CAPE AND HARRISON SMITH, INCORPORATED,
139 EAST 46TH STREET, NEW YORK, N. Y. AND 77 WELLINGTON
STREET, WEST, TORONTO, CANADA; JONATHAN CAPE, LTD.,
30 BEDFORD SQUARE, LONDON, W. C. 1, ENGLAND

OUR NEW RELIGION

AN EXAMINATION OF
CHRISTIAN SCIENCE

H. A. L. FISHER

NEW YORK
JONATHAN CAPE & HARRISON SMITH

THE TRUTH SEEKER
Box 2832
San Diego, Calif. U.S.A. 92112

COPYRIGHT, 1930, BY
JONATHAN CAPE AND HARRISON SMITH
INCORPORATED

FIRST PUBLISHED IN AMERICA 1930

PRINTED IN THE UNITED STATES OF AMERICA
BY J. J. LITTLE & IVES CO.
AND BOUND BY THE J. F. TAPLEY CO.

CONTENTS

I   THE PROPHETESS   1

II THE CREED   83

III THE CHURCH   131

I

THE PROPHETESS

"I'm going home! Home to the land where sects are as the sands of the seashore, and no belief is too queer to become a cult."—STEPHEN DUGGAN.

THE PROPHETESS

NORTH AMERICA is the land of new religions. We find here, as in Asia Minor in the second century of the Christian era, an intellectual and emotional soil wonderfully adapted for the growth of religious experiences and enterprises. No belief is too wild, too crude, or too fantastic to prevent its acceptance by some section or other of the vast, miscellaneous, and mobile population which inhabits this continent. As the power of institutional religion is weak and education in the main superficial, vagaries of the religious imagination, which the discipline of the Church might coerce or the criticism of the intellect dissolve, are found to flourish in tropical abundance. Some of these creeds have the short life of a butterfly; they spring up, sun themselves for a moment, and then disappear into everlasting darkness. Others, responding to some larger or more substantial need of the human heart, make converts, create institutions, and survive the men and women to whose original impulse they owe their existence. Of these more permanent manifestations of the American religious impulse, by far the most remarkable, judged by the width of its appeal and the extent of the material resources at its command, is Christian Science.

The founder of this movement was a woman who combined in her own person many characteristic qualities of the North American people. She was a sincere, though quite uncritical student of the Bible. The wife of three husbands, she wrote a Best Seller, launched some successful newspapers, and died leaving nearly three million dollars, all made out of religion. Judged by its external tests, no career could be more successful. Long before Mary Baker Eddy "passed out of the flesh," she was the recipient of semi-divine honours, a source of legend, and the centre of a mythology. A great church in Boston was erected for the conduct of Christian Science worship, and decorated with affectionate munificence by her admiring disciples. A special shrine, known as "The Mother's Room," was remarkable for an onyx mantelpiece of opalescent green, an onyx table, a large china lamp and shade, an Assyrian bridal veil, silvery-green plush draperies and antique Persian rugs, a handkerchief, a tiny pincushion, dressing-gown, slippers, and a large oil painting (a gift from the Reverend Mother herself) of the little rocking-chair covered in black haircloth in which she sat while writing *Science and Health*.

To the zealots of the faith hers was a figure hardly less holy and significant than the person of Jesus Himself. Had she not restored the lost art of Christian healing? Was she not appointed to illumine for the world the female aspect of the godhead? Was it not her mission to complete the message of Christ, and to add to those old Scriptures composed so long ago, so far away, and in languages so unfamiliar, a modern supplement, more intelligible, more actual, more closely adjusted to the practical needs of man? Miss Sibyl Wilbur, her authorised biographer, does not affect to conceal the place which Mary Baker Eddy holds among the sacred loyalties of the devout. That gallant American lady compares herself to the author of the earliest Synoptic Gospel. "I place myself," she writes, "unreservedly on the methods of St. Mark." Miss Wilbur's piety is beyond reproach, and if her style is not that of the Evangelist, the discrepancy, should it attract the notice of the faithful, will be certain to escape their censure.

There is nothing romantic about the origin of the prophetess. She was born on July 16th, 1821, in a plain substantial farmhouse overlooking the broad valley of the Merrimac and situated in the township of Bow, New Hampshire. Her father was a thriving yeoman of the name of Baker, whose family had been settled for six generations in those pleasant fields and uplands of Puritan New England. A devout sharp-tempered Calvinist, surer of hell fire than of his crops and seasons, he believed in its extreme form the awful doctrine that the majority of the human race were destined to eternal damnation. From this dark and forbidding view of human destiny a serene and cultivated wife and six healthy children, three of either sex, failed to detach him. Then a seventh child was born. She was a girl, and received the name of Mary.

The child was studious and hysterical. "Now she would fall headlong to the floor writhing and screaming in apparent agony. At other times she became rigid like a cataleptic and continued for some time in a state of suspended animation." Dr. Ladd, the village physician, diagnosed "hysteria mingled with bad temper"; but, whatever may have been the moral and physical root of these convulsive disorders, they spared Mary the roughening routine of the district school, and gave her space for dreams and meditation. She read Thomson's *Seasons,* wrote melancholy little verses, and resolved to become a great authoress. Above all else, she read and re-read the Bible. Finding that David prayed three times daily, she determined to do likewise. In her ninth year she heard voices. Was it a symptom of overstrain, as her fond relatives imagined, or a Divine call, as the devout were subsequently disposed to imagine? In any case, she was no tame recipient of the family theology. At the age of twelve she tells us that she declared war on the paternal doctrine of unconditional election, and embarked on a struggle with her obstinate father which reduced her to a bed of sickness. A mother's loving care, we are given to understand, was of more avail in effecting a cure than the medicines of the physician. "My mother, as she bathed my burning temples, bade me lean on God's love, which would give me rest if I went to Him in prayer, as I was wont to do. Seeking His guidance, I prayed: and a soft glow of ineffable joy came over me. The fever was gone and I rose and dressed myself, in a normal condition of health. Mother saw this and was glad. The physicians marvelled, and the 'horrible decree' of predestination—as John Calvin rightly called his own tenet—for ever lost its power over me."

In a word, an instance of faith cure and a premonition of the Church of Christ Scientist. Every familiar ingredient of the Christian Science miracle is present—the inefficiency of medicine, the power and instantaneous healing effect of prayer, the amazement of the physicians, the profound and permanent spiritual consequence of a change accomplished by spiritual means. All autobiography is a mixture of truth and falsehood; and, in throwing back into early childhood an experience to support her later theories, the prophetess of the New Religion may have suffered from one of the commonest forms of self-deception which beset the human mind.

Persons subject to hysteria make bad witnesses. Long afterwards, when this little girl was famous and middle-aged, it became natural to her and to her admirers to find analogies between the lives of Christ and of the prophetess who had revealed to the modern world the lost art of Christian healing. At the age of twelve Christ had confounded the doctors in the Temple. Whom had Mrs. Eddy confounded at the age of twelve? The answer was that she had confounded her father by denying predestination and the members of the Congregational Church at Tilton by refusing, upon her admission, to accept the doctrine of transubstantiation. The autobiography of the saint is not immune from error. Mary Baker, as the records show, was, at the time of her admission to the Congregational Church at Tilton, not twelve, but seventeen years of age.

Tilton (or Sanbornton Bridge, as it was then called) was a little New Hampshire country town into the neighbourhood of which Mary's parents removed when she was in her fifteenth year. Here was Dr. Sanborn's academy for girls, and a Sunday school, and the Rev. Enoch Corser, a benevolent silver-haired Congregationalist minister with a leonine head and shaggy eyebrows and strong views on the value of hell fire, and here, too, was a sufficient supply of marriageable young men. Mary Baker, like her sisters, was good-looking. As she taught in the Sunday school she aroused the admiration of the children for her becoming clothes, her gloves, her fine cambric handkerchief, her sweet musical voice and little affectations of speech and manner, her deep-set blue eyes (or were they grey?) and chestnut hair. At Dr. Sanborn's academy she continued her broken studies, and was supplied with a training in rhetoric which was probably less deleterious to the mind than the vague smattering of metaphysics which she had acquired from a premature participation, at the age of twelve, in the undergraduate studies of an elder brother. Walks and talks with the Rev. Enoch Corser furnished the religious side of her education. "One can picture them," writes Miss Wilbur (after the manner of St. Mark), "of a fine summer evening, the slender girl and the old scholar, in their usual promenade in the garden. . . . As she looked up at her pastor her great blue eyes poured sunshine upon him, and she smiled with such radiance that he was struck dumb in the midst of his defence of Hades." To the many reasons for challenging Dr. Corser's pessimism there was soon to be added a very special reason in the shape of Mr. George Washington Glover, who had been associated with brother Samuel Baker in his business of contractor and builder in Boston and was now established at Charleston, South Carolina. Mr. or Colonel Glover (for are not all male Virginians colonels?) fell in love with Mary Baker, and was married to her two weeks before the Christmas of 1843.

The life of a building contractor owning slaves and struggling for dollars cannot fail to provide problems for a religious nature. Mrs. Glover was repelled by the institution of slavery, but to Colonel George Washington Glover, living in Charleston, where all employers owned slaves, and emancipation was expressly prohibited by law, business was business and slaves were money. The entreaties of the tender young wife were waved aside by the bustling young husband; but fate has its own ironic way of settling the controversies of mankind. A cathedral was required for the coloured population of Haiti. Colonel Glover, hot upon the discharge of a lucrative contract, was struck down by the yellow fever at Wilmington, and an untimely widowhood was followed by a surreptitious emancipation.

Returning to her father's home, the young widow gave birth to a son, a physical trial which gravely affected a constitution that was never robust. To spinal trouble, causing spasmodic seizures which were followed by prostrations, there were now superadded other evils—the loss of a husband's property, the death of a cherished mother, the remarriage of a father, and the banishment of a child.

The circumstances under which Mrs. Glover was separated from her boy have never been entirely cleared up. That Mark Baker's new wife should not have cared to have her husband's grandson in the house is quite understandable; but soon after Mark Baker's remarriage Mrs. Glover had removed to the house of her elder sister. It is difficult to believe that Abigail Tilton, the wife of a wealthy manufacturer, could not have found room for her sister's child, seeing that she had but two children of her own, a girl and a boy. It is possible that the presence of a noisy little boy was deemed to be bad for the nerves of a sensitive invalid; perhaps also that the nervous imaginings of the mother were not altogether wholesome for the son. But if there is anything certain about the character of our heroine it is that she was a woman of determined will and autocratic temper. Nobody can doubt that if Mrs. Glover had wanted to keep her child with her she would have found means of doing so. It was the family view that she wanted no such thing, that she had conceived a nervous distaste of the child herself. "Mary," they said, "acts like an old ewe that won't own its lamb. She won't have the boy near her." Whatever the reason may be, the painful severance was effected, and the pen of the bereaved mother, desisting from its contributions to abolitionist literature, found relief in some verses entitled "Mother's Darling," of which the following quatrain was subsequently recalled to the memory of her admirers by a not dissatisfied authoress:

> Their smile through tears, as sunshine on the sea
> Awakes new beauty in the surge's roll!
> Oh, life is dead, bereft of all, with thee—
> Star of my earthly hope, hope of my soul.

The interesting widow, something of a poet, something of a Blue Stocking, something of a spiritualist, something of a politician—for she held and courageously expressed strong anti-slavery views—was not long left without a male admirer. Among the kinsmen of her new stepmother was Dr. Daniel Patterson, dentist and homœopathist, who descried in the invalid lady, with her wayward ailments and well-to-do relatives, an interesting patient and a hopeful wife. Dr. Patterson was a big, handsome, vulgar man, lavish in his attentions to women, and with a florid taste in costume, which led him to carry his silk hat and kid gloves into remote country villages. His cheery confidence vanquished all obstacles. He used the arguments most likely to tell with a lady very anxious about her health and often fretting for her absent child. A course of homœopathy would expel the disease, and as for the boy, nothing would be easier, once they were married, than to settle in the neighbourhood of Groton, where the little George Glover was now, under the tutelage of an affectionate nurse, unfolding the resources of a boisterous and not too pleasant disposition. The suit prospered, and in 1850 Mary Glover, *née* Baker, then in the thirtieth year of her age, was married to her handsome and exuberant dentist.

The homœopathy and the marriage were alike failures. Further acquaintance with the showy Dr. Patterson disclosed some serious defects of character. He was too attentive to the ladies, too neglectful of affairs. He was, in fact, sold up. Moreover, he cannot be said to have implemented the undertakings with respect to the boy George which he appears to have made during the period of his courtship.

The Pattersons, indeed, did move to Groton in 1856, presumably in order to be near the boy; but the visits of George were not agreeable. Dr. Patterson, probably at his wife's instigation, reported to Abigail Tilton that the boy exhausted his mother; and again the family influence was brought to bear to secure a separation; this time with decisive success, for it was not until he had reached the age of thirty-four, and was the father of two children, that his mother once more set eyes upon her son.

Was Mrs. Patterson a reluctant or a passive victim of these proceedings? Was there, counterworking the emotions of a mother's heart, the feeling that perhaps after all, this noisy and very healthy little boy might not be the best thing for her precious health? The official explanations of this episode, given long afterwards by the famous religious heroine, are certainly curious. We are asked to believe that the boy was spirited away from his mother by some malign conspiracy, that he was removed to a region in the west whither he could not be traced, that he was falsely informed of his mother's death and supplied with a strange guardian, and that in all this sinister tragedy Dr. Patterson was in some shadowy way a consenting, if not a shaping, figure. Poor Dr. Patterson! To protect the slumbers of an exacting invalid how often had he not been sent out into the night to wage a forlorn campaign against croaking frogs! If he thought, as well he may, that for nerves so delicately spun and a temper so easily frayed, a boy in the home is even worse than a frog in the brook, who will greatly blame him? But Dr. Patterson was one of those luckless mortals who can do nothing right.

Even the Civil War, which reversed so many reputations, did not alter Dr. Patterson's name for infelicity. He must needs visit battles, not as a dentist nor as a combatant, but out of the curiosity of a tourist. And so one day, being pleasantly interested in the battle of Bull Run, and venturing too far in the direction of his opponents, he fell into enemy hands, and for the remaining two years of the war found rest alike from his practice and his wife in a Southern gaol. For a second time Mary Baker was set to face the world alone.

How could she feel a sense of impoverishment at the loss of her uncongenial consort? Mary Baker was very closely engaged with her own important problems, spiritual and physical. Never, even in her least fantastic moments, had she regarded herself as a creature moulded from the common clay. She was peculiar, with a soul and body which set her apart from and above her neighbours. She went into trances, and saw visions. In a society vividly interested in spiritualism, she made pretensions to clairvoyance, acted as a medium, and was even so daring as to indicate the spot at which Captain Kidd's treasure would be unearthed. What if the treasure hunters were disappointed in their quest? Mary Baker remained to herself and to others an unusual, an arresting phenomenon. Her privileged communications with the other world, sometimes misleading but always impressive, her contributions in prose and verse to the local papers, the unusual and interesting character of her spinal ailments, so baffling to science, her air of authority and self-esteem, combined to secure for her a social importance with unfurnished and credulous minds. She was above all things engaged with problems of her own physical health. How could she shake off these vague, persistent ailments? Expedient chased expedient through her busy and curious brain. To live suspended in a cradle, made to order and rocked by sedulous hands, how would that do? So a cradle was constructed, and for a time cradle-rocking became, not only a family, but a village occupation. A diet of coarse bread and fruit and a nightly rub down in alcohol? That too was tried, without success. Dr. Vail's famous water cure at Hill, taken on the special recommendation of Abigail Tilton? Failure followed failure. Finally she had recourse to a man of dubious reputation to whom Dr. Patterson had, on October 14th, 1861, furnished the particulars of her complaint, in the hope that, where all others had failed, he, by his new and unorthodox methods, might achieve success.

Phineas P. Quimby was one of those adventurers, more common perhaps in the New World than the Old, who, navigating the sea of knowledge without the charts and compass of education, end always by discovering to their own intimate satisfaction results which have eluded the wisdom of the ages. Quimby was the son of a blacksmith. In early manhood he had displayed ingenuity and inventiveness as a watchmaker. Then, excited by the exploits of Charles Poyen, a travelling French mesmerist, he discovered in himself an unusual degree of mesmeric power, toured the country with a boy medium, and built up a flourishing practice as a healer. Though he was small and slight, everything about him denoted energy, decision, and the best intentions. His forehead was high, his quick black eyes full of kindness and intelligence, his small body highly charged with nervous force. Being entirely self-taught, he possessed all the pride of the autodidact. He believed in himself, and succeeded in communicating his confidence to an ever-widening circle of patients. At first he had laid stress upon the services of his medium to diagnose disorders and to prescribe appropriate remedies. Later he found that the medium could be dispensed with, and if, upon occasions, clairvoyance and mesmerism were still employed, it was not from a continuing belief in their efficacy, but as a concession to the frailty of the patient.

Some time before Mary Baker's visit to Portland, Quimby, now a grey-haired man of sixty, had come to the conclusion that there was only one cure for all diseases, the confidence of the patient in the healer. "My practice," he said, "is unlike all medical practice. I give no medicine, and make no outward applications. I tell the patient his troubles, and what he thinks is his disease, and my explanation is the cure. If I succeed in correcting his errors, I change the fluids of the system, and establish the faith in health. The Truth is the cure." So he would sit by his patients, read their thoughts, and persuade them to think that their ailments were in some part of the body other than that which was in fact affected. He also at times employed clairvoyance in diagnosis, and rubbed the head and body, and sent his patient into a mesmeric sleep. By these means he undoubtedly effected cures, and, being a resourceful and clever man, invented an absurd theory of health and disease to explain them.

When Mary Baker presented herself in October 1862 at the International Hotel, Portland, Maine, the popular healer sat down by her, told her that her animal spirit was reflecting its grief upon her body and calling it spinal disease. He then dipped his hands in water, rubbed her head violently, and sent her into a mesmeric sleep. She awoke cured of her pain. The next day the treatment was repeated, with the same astonishing and gratifying result. Nor was there a relapse. The cure appeared to be as permanent as it was swift. How had it been effected? The patient (if we may trust an account written nearly thirty years afterwards) had no doubt as to the sources of Mr. Quimby's power. "It is not magnetism which does this work, Doctor. You have no need to touch me, nor disorder my hair with your mesmeric passes." "What then do you think does the healing?" he asked. "Your knowledge of God's law, your understanding of the truth which Christ brought into the world and which had been lost for ages."

Unfortunately, Mr. Quimby was an unbeliever.[1]

One thing was evident. Mrs. Patterson's spinal disease was so far exorcised that she tripped up a hundred and eighty-two steps to the Dome of the City Hall to proclaim to the world the greatness of Quimby. For, despite his profession of atheism, she believed in Quimby, insisting, in the face of reiterated protestations, that Quimby was the vessel of the divine purpose, that magnetism and clairvoyance had nothing whatever to do with his success, and that mind healing through faith in God was the sole and sufficient explanation of the apparent miracle. Before this enthusiastic advocacy Mr. Quimby thought well to beat a retreat. If the dear, overwhelming lady would insist in comparing him to the Founder of Christianity, it was not for him to kick against the pricks. The analogy might be remote, but it might also be convenient. There were patients who might be gratified in reflecting as he ruffled their hair in the morning, or as they sat unruffling it in the afternoon,

---

[1] This allegation, proceeding from Mrs. Eddy, is violently contested by Quimby's friends, but is, on the whole, sustained by a study of the Quimby MSS. published in 1921.

that they were touched by an emanation of the Divine Spirit. An aroma of sanctity, ill as it accorded with his own temperament and convictions, might attract a new class of patient and justify higher fees. Perhaps magnetism, after all, was not so important; perhaps, after all, matter was not everything, and there might be something in the insistent eloquence of the lady who wrote to the local newspapers comparing him to Jesus Christ. Without abandoning his older methods, to which, even before Mrs. Patterson's appearance, he had ceased to attach a serious importance, Mr. Quimby was prepared, with a mild protest (*"A defence against making myself equal to Christ"*), to wear the unsolicited halo and to turn it to the best professional account; but the profane vulgar discovered incongruities. In Portland the public "fairly caught its breath," and exclaimed (in the language of the hagiographer), "What, this Quimby compared to Christ! What next?"

Mrs. Patterson had no doubt as to what should follow next. Mr. Quimby should write a great book upon the science of healing, setting out the true principles, hitherto concealed from mortals, for the preservation of health and the cure of disease. Now Mr. Quimby was not what is termed a literary man. Though he was fond of scribbling his thoughts in a copy-book, and could scribble with rapidity when he was about it, punctuation, orthography, and the use of capitals were foreign to his practice. Neither by discipline nor by devotion was he equipped for the ambitious rôle designed for him by his devoted patient. He held that religious beliefs were founded in deception. Mrs. Patterson was an earnest advocate of the view that religion was all in all, and that matter, if not outside the category of being was at least irrelevant. Mr. Quimby jotted down reflections on his cases; Mrs. Patterson embroidered her own reflections on Mr. Quimby's reflections. The gentleman was confused; the lady was by no means clear; and the attempt to found upon the Quimby cures a philosophy of healing equally compatible with Quimby's own processes and convictions, and the very opposite religious preconceptions entertained by his lady friend and literary coadjutor, was by no means an easy task. Nevertheless, to Quimby's satisfaction some literature was circulated in manuscript for the edification of his patients.

To Mrs. Patterson nothing was at the moment so important as to define, to preach, and to promote the Quimby system. She gave lectures on Quimby; she wrote articles on Quimby; she indited poems to Quimby; she employed the resources of her industrious pen in contriving a philosophy for Quimby. The open scepticism of her sister, Mrs. Tilton, who tried Quimbyism on an unsatisfactory son and found it unavailing against alcohol and tobacco, did not deter her. So long as Quimby lived, Mrs. Patterson was an admiring, faithful, and, so far as strictly contemporary record goes, quite uncritical disciple.

"Mid light of science sits the sage profound," she observes in a complimentary sonnet. Even in absence, the science of the sage —"the Christian Science," as he was sometimes moved to call it—was tremulously invoked, and thanks recorded for "angel visits," visits effectual, not only against the grave disorders of the flesh, but even against "small beliefs" (for what, asked Mr. Quimby, was disease but erroneous belief?) such as "stomach trouble, backache, and constipation."

From these solemn occupations Mrs. Patterson was briefly diverted by the reappearance of a husband. Two years of a Southern prison had effected little change in the ebullient dentist. He was still as restless, as superficial and as flighty as ever. Hardly was he restored to the bosom of his family but he was off upon a long tour, lecturing on his Southern experiences. At last he was prevailed upon to settle down, to make a home for his wife, and to endeavour once again to build up a dental and medical practice. The Pattersons established themselves at Lynn, a flourishing centre of the boot and shoe industry in the proximity of Boston, which, in the courageous scriptures of the new religion, is likened to the shores of the Lake of Galilee. Here Dr. Patterson discovered an interest remote alike from his professional duties and from the religious meditations of a too earnest consort. He fell in love, and, decamping with the daughter of an opulent patient, left the philosopher of his hearthside to face the world alone on a scanty allowance of two hundred dollars a year.

The flight of Dr. Patterson, temporarily inconvenient and perhaps distressing as it may have been, made no difference to the general flow of his wife's activities. The disappearance of Mr. Quimby, who died early in 1866 of an ulcer in the stomach, which neither clairvoyance, nor magnetism, nor mind healing could remove, was a far more important event. Quimby eliminated, the way was open for Quimby's disciple to unfold at will what she conceived to be the true as opposed to the erroneous elements of the great master's doctrine. The date of Mr. Quimby's death is, therefore, by no obscure chain of causation, the date of the birth of Christian Science. But as philosophies arise out of wonder, so religions spring out of miracle. A mere development of doctrine, such as it is the task of rationalising historians to record, has no spectacular value. The truth of a new faith must be confirmed by a miraculous cure. Such a miracle was fortunately forthcoming at the psychological moment to illustrate the origins of Christian Science.

It was in Massachusetts, in February 1866, and after the death of the magnetic doctor, Mr. P. P. Quimby,

THE PROPHETESS

whom spiritualists would associate therewith, but who was in no wise connected with this event, that I discovered the science of divine metaphysical healing which I afterwards named Christian Science. The discovery came to pass in this way. During twenty years prior to my discovery I had been trying to trace all physical effects to a mental cause; and in the latter part of 1866 I gained the scientific certainty that all causation was Mind, and every effect a mental phenomenon.

My immediate recovery from the effects of an injury caused by an accident, an injury that neither medicine nor surgery could reach, was the falling apple that led me to the discovery how to be well myself, and how to make others so.

Even to the homeopathic physician who attended me, and rejoiced in my recovery, I could not then explain the *modus* of my relief. I could only assure him that the Divine Spirit had wrough the miracle—a miracle which later I found to be in perfect scientific accord with divine law.

"The injury which neither medicine nor surgery could reach" was caused by an accident which was thus reported in the *Lynn Reporter* of February 3rd, 1866:

Mrs. Mary Patterson of Swampscott (a suburb of Lynn) fell upon the ice near the corner of Market and Oxford Streets on Thursday evening and was severely injured. She was taken up in an insensible condition and carried into the residence of S. M. Bubier, Esq., near by, where she was kindly cared for during the night. Dr. Cushing, who was called, found her injuries to be internal and of a severe nature, inducing spasms and internal suffering. She was removed to her home in Swampscott yesterday afternoon, though in a very critical condition.

It appears that Dr. Cushing had said little, but that "his face and manner conveyed more than his words"; enough, in any case, to justify the communication of one of those sombre and alarming paragraphs which the reporter of a local paper expects to receive and friends and relations are delighted to furnish. In fact, Dr. Cushing diagnosed the case as one of concussion, possibly accompanied by spinal dislocation. "I found her," he says, "very nervous, partially unconscious, semi-hysterical, complaining by word and action of severe pain in the back of her head and neck." He prescribed some mild remedies, the third decimal alternation of arnica, and afterwards one-eighth of a grain of morphine, and does not appear to have been surprised at the patient's recovery. Being interrogated by Miss Wilbur in 1907, he stated that he did not remember being told at the time of a miraculous cure through the power of prayer.

Far otherwise were the impressions communicated to the world more than twenty

THE PROPHETESS

years after the event by the Founder of Christian Science. "The miracle of the fall at Lynn" had now long become an article of an established faith, a cornerstone of the True Church, an *experimentum crucis,* pure of disturbing factors, upon which the remedial efficacy of prayer could be securely based. The inconvenient circumstance that a distinguished medical practitioner had been called in, that he had attended the patient on four successive days, that he had prescribed medicines and an opiate, that his medicines and opiates had been taken, could not be altogether denied; but it was contended that the doctor had not been summoned by the patient's will, that his remedies were wholly inadequate to effect a cure, and that the dose prescribed for the second day had been heroically declined. Mrs. Eddy, as by this time she was called, does not minimise her heroism in declining, as after twenty-five years she thinks she did, to empty Dr. Cushing's bottle. "The miracles recorded in the Bible," she writes, "which had before seemed to me supernatural, grew divinely natural and apprehensible. Adoringly I discovered the Principle of His holy heroism and Christian example on the cross when He refused to drink the 'vinegar and gall,' a preparation of poppy or aconite to allay the tortures of crucifixion."

Time has its own transforming alchemy. As time went on, the cure at Lynn, despite the annoying intervention of Dr. Cushing, with his opiates and medicines, was taken to supply the definitive proof of the new religion and art of healing, and vested with properties of increasing importance for the history of mankind. "In the year 1866," observes the prophetess, "I discovered the Christ Science, or Divine Laws of Life, Truth, and Love, and named my discovery Christian Science." The evidence of this portentous revelation was supplied by the fall at Lynn. "Dr. Cushing pronounced my injury incurable, and that I could not survive three days because of it." Dr. Cushing, who was afterwards called in to treat Mrs. Patterson for a cough, denies in terms that he ever made the statement attributed to him.

The historical student is entitled to doubt whether at this epoch of her life Mary Baker was as firmly established in her subsequent faith as she afterwards professed to be. Had she altogether abandoned magnetism, seeing that her pupils continued to rub the heads of their patients till 1872? Did she or did she not still repose some lingering faith in spiritualism? Were the absurd letters written to Mrs. Crosby, in which she pretended to personate the spirit of her dead brother Albert, merely a practical joke, devised to laugh a silly woman out of her spiritual follies? Or are they capable of another interpretation? Was Mrs. Patterson, the guest in a spiritualist household, endeavouring to impress her hostess with the communications which a gifted sister could establish with a brother's ghost? We incline with Mrs. Crosby, who received and subsequently published these letters, to the latter hypothesis, for the parent of Christian Science was not prone to jests, but, like the solicitor in *Pendennis,* "by profession a serious person."

The faith-healing of Lynn is now the consecrated doctrine of a wealthy Church. Yet the natal year of Christian Science has not always been assigned to 1866, nor the cure at Lynn linked with it as an evidential miracle.

Mythologies do not spring from the ground full grown. They develop from the seed, taking shape and colour from the circumambient air, and waxing with each successive relaxation of critical pressure. Only after three earlier dates had been propounded and discarded did the Founder of Christian Science decide to discover in 1866 the natal year of the new religion. Only many years after she had paid his bill did she venture to publish the fact that Dr. Cushing had declared her illness incurable. It is at least noteworthy that, writing a fortnight after the accident to Mr. Dresser, a fellow-pupil of Quimby's, and specially interested in mind healing, she made no reference to a miraculous recovery.

However this may be, there is no reason to doubt that the accretions of spiritualism and magnetism were beginning to fall away from the central core of a doctrine which found in Christian faith the sole and sovereign remedy for the imagined pains of mankind. But the world still remained cold and sceptical. Sister Abigail (Mrs. Tilton) was a thoroughgoing Philistine, and would have nothing to do with sister Mary's eccentricities. Ellen Pilsbury roundly denied that she had benefited by Aunt Mary's cure. To the well-to-do people like the Winslows the lady healer appeared to be chasing a delusion.

The manner of her life during the three years which followed the cure at Lynn is something of a mystery. She flits from one obscure lodging-house to another. She makes a convert of Hiram S. Crafts, a heel-finisher, and for some time lives in his humble household until tiffs with Mrs. Crafts, a spiritualist, drive her afield. She stays with Mrs. Webster, a silly old lady who owns a "spiritualist room" and "spiritualist furniture," until she is ejected for her revolutionary opinions by Mrs. Webster's son, who has no mind for seeing his holiday spoiled by perpetual perorations to promote a cause of which he heartily disapproves. Many of her hostesses are spiritualists, for spiritualism was a fashionable creed in Massachusetts. Meanwhile she was steadily writing. A public library was unneeded. It was sufficient to own the Bible and her Quimby note-books, for she had set herself the task of commenting on the Scriptures in the light of her new-found belief.

In the early stages of her career as a healer, and while her ambitious literary work was still on the anvil, she did not scruple to acknowledge her indebtedness to Quimby. She would, says Mrs. Wentworth, her hostess in 1869, fold her hands on her lap, tilt her head on one side, and, gently nodding, explain in mincing tones, "I learnt this from Dr. Quimby, and he made me promise to teach it to at least two persons before I die." She taught also from a Quimby manuscript. It was not until long afterwards, when her book was famous and she had become the head of a flourishing sect, that she proclaimed her complete independence of Quimby's teaching. Although confronted with the letters and addresses in which, in the first flush of her grateful enthusiasm, she had lauded Quimby to the skies, she replied that her old master had placed her under a mesmeric spell, and that she was not to be held accountable for anything which she had then written in his praise.

Gratitude and honesty are flowers which seldom grow upon the soil of a nature at once hysterical and ambitious. If our heroine fell short of the ordinary standards of intellectual integrity, if she was not above repudiating an intellectual debt, if in the later stages of a successful life she was brought to see her past through a glaze of sentiment, and to regard herself as a figure sweet and saintly, original and inspired, exposed to great and malignant tribulations, but marked out by God from the first as a chosen vessel of his sublime purpose, we need not blame her overmuch. A popular leader is always something of a charlatan, an autobiographer something of a poet; and the powers of self-deception accorded to the hysterical are acknowledged to be great. It is, then, no matter for surprise that Quimby was repudiated by the disciple who by ceaseless labouring had so worked his directing idea into her life that, combining with genuine religious sentiments and a strong foundation of self-esteem, it almost appeared to be an original part of her being. What exactly her book owes to Quimby remains, and will probably continue to remain, a matter of doubt: nor does it much signify. If *Science and Health* would never have been written without Quimby, Quimby would certainly never have written *Science and Health;* and in the development of Christian Science that book, and that book only, has been of decisive importance. Even if the guiding thoughts were derived from Quimby's teaching, it was only after they had passed through the dim, twisting corridors of Mary Baker's mind, and had flowed out as a force operating upon her dominating will and shaping her impetuous and sustained activities, that the world began to take note of them. So some astute firm exploits the discovery of the scientific recluse, and makes for it a new and transformed life in the thoroughfares of business.[1]

In the scale of her ambition the pupil was fully a match for her master. Quimby, as is now made clear from his published notebooks, believed himself to be in possession of a secret of profound significance for mankind. Mary Baker was confident that to her it had been vouchsafed to discern the true meaning of that secret, and to make it available for the spiritual guidance of humanity as a doctrine of revolutionary and decisive importance.

[1] "The scientific man or man outside matter," a phrase occurring in the Quimby MSS., anticipates, both in thought and language, a cardinal principle of Christian Science.—Dresser, *The Quimby MSS.*, p. 236.

Nor, if we take account of the curious spiritual atmosphere of New England at that time, is it altogether surprising that a woman so ill-furnished should have come forward with a panacea for all human ills. It was an age of Messianic pretensions and of wild beliefs and expectations, some new and revolutionary, others old, even primitive, such as that all illness is of diabolic origin, or that men communicate with the spirit world, or that by some refinement of nature or clever expedient, such as a particular method of respiration, it might be possible to escape old age and death. The idea that God was both male and female, and that Christ had been incarnated a second time in the person of a certain Mary Lee, was fervently held by the Shakers, a religious sect established in the neighbourhood of Bow, and well known to the Founder of Christian Science. In 1861, Frank Howland, a youth in Massachusetts, decided that he was immortal, and obtained adherents. If disease was the work of the Devil, then the man who was thoroughly purged of the Devil could defy illness, old age, and death. Such ideas floating in the brain of the common people created a feeling that at any moment some unexpected glory and deliverance might be made known to men.

The mind which Mary Baker Patterson brought to the service of her literary ambitions was of a curious and unusual calibre. Entirely unchastened by converse with the intellectual world—for she had seen no company but that of her intellectual inferiors—impervious to the ordinary canons of evidence, apprehending only those facts which complied with its preconceptions, and blind to every countervailing consideration, full of those obscurities and confusions which beset the amateur of mediocre intelligence who ventures to treat of the ultimate problems of life and knowledge, it was nevertheless characterised by some remarkable qualities. Without dialectical ability it was cast in a metaphysical mould. It was a universalising mind, governed by a natural impulse to search for ultimate causes and relations and to see in the particular facts of experience the illustration of some wider principle. It was, therefore, despite all its deficiencies on the side of clarity and elegance and logical gift, a mind of a certain power, and calculated to impress persons unversed in the art of detecting intellectual sophistries, the more so since she was not one of those philosophers who, when they go abroad, leave their philosophy behind them under lock and key. The doctrine followed the doctrinaire like a shadow. She could not sit down to strawberries and cream without observing that "some day Christian Science will enable us to enjoy such a treat without raising the fruit, compounding the cake, pressing the cream, or buying the sugar."

Moreover, she was a religious woman. If the metaphysical promptings of her mind impelled her to search for a system of the universe, the religious side of it gave to that system its emotional quality and content. Prayer, meditation, eager and puzzled interrogation of the Bible, had claimed from childhood much of her energy, so that those who met her in later times were conscious of a certain quiet exaltation, such as may come to a woman nursing a secret spiritual advantage. Again, she was sentimental. When she writes about spring—and she abounds in effusions about birds and trees and the glories of Nature—she can say nothing simply. "The cuckoo sounds her viewless flute to call the feathered tribes back from their winter residences." She cannot tell us what she thinks it right to feel about the cuckoo at any slighter expense of her imposing but always unfortunate vocabulary. Yet in the leadership of a religious movement sentiment counts for much, and Mary Baker's commonplace but quite genuine vein of gushing sentiment about religion and the ocean and the sunset and the cuckoo was of the exact quality to commend her message to that simple audience in the eastern states of the American Union to whom it was originally addressed.

Further, her mind, though slovenly, was purposive and audacious. Many admirable intelligences fail to make an impression upon the world for the lack of any central system of illumination. This was not the case with Mary Baker. That dominating middle-aged lady, who passed from lodging-house to lodging-house, scribbling indefatigably at her *magnum opus,* and steadily improving her little fortune by courses of instruction in her

THE PROPHETESS

new art of healing, was illumined by an idea, containing real elements of truth and value, which supplied a direction to all her activities. She believed that a spiritual life transcending the human formed the ultimate basis of reality. She saw that pain was a state of consciousness. She believed that pain could therefore be cured by superinducing another state of consciousness without the intervention of material agents. She thought that mind was everything and matter nothing. Searching the Scriptures, she found that Christ was a healer who effected His cures, not by material drugs, but by spiritual influence. She found also that Christ had directed His disciples to heal, but that, after the death of its Founder, the Church had lost its hold over the art of Christian healing, with the result that a large amount of unnecessary pain and evil had been caused to humanity. She believed that under the inscrutable will of Providence it had been reserved for her to restore the vanished art of Christian healing, and to demonstrate to the world that illness and pain and sin would yield to the medicaments of Christian faith. Sustained by this confidence, she persevered in her task with a resolution which all the sordid and depressing circumstances of her outer life were unable to shake.

A personal creed is one thing. A scientific patent is another. How could a creed be converted into a patent? How could mind-healing, a territory so indefinite in its outlines, shading here into mesmerism, there into spiritualism, be delimited, appropriated, converted into a commercial proposition and an institutional fact? The answer to this question lay at hand in the religious experience of Puritan New England. The Puritans among whom Mary Baker grew up were children of the Book. They believed the Bible to contain the Word of God. Every sentence, every word, every syllable of the Bible was true and charged with sacred meaning; everything written elsewhere which conflicted with the authorised text was palpably false. The scruples and doubts and critical objections raised by the Higher Criticism were unfamiliar to these simple folk. They knew nothing of the theologians of Tübingen; they had heard no breath of doctrine directed against the literal truth of the Holy Writ. But the

THE PROPHETESS 45

Bible was an old book. It had not been written in America. Much of its phraseology was obscure, many of its allusions were difficult. It was true in every jot and tittle if suitably interpreted, but it could not be said to be up to date. It needed a supplement—an American supplement—equally authoritative, equally sacred, equally inspired, a supplement on the science and art of Christian healing, protected with all the safeguards which the Copyright Acts could supply, and serving alike as a depository of the true faith and a patent cure for physical disease. Colleges might fall into heresy, professors and lecturers might go astray. The Book of the inspired Teacher, the fruit of a new immaculate conception, would not err.

The importance of the book as a patent, valuable alike on spiritual and economic grounds, was not at once perceived. For many years Mary Baker, over and above her literary activities, carried on work as a healer and as a teacher of the healing art. For these services she was entitled to charge a fee. A course of twelve lessons was originally given for a hundred dollars, payable in advance, plus a ten per cent commission on the profits of teaching and healing; but later on the fee was trebled, and the course of lectures reduced from twelve to seven.

> When God impelled me to set a price on my instruction in Christian mind-healing, I could think of no financial equivalent for an impartation of a knowledge of that Divine power which heals; but I was led to name three hundred dollars as the price for each pupil in one course of lessons at my college—a startling sum for tuition lasting barely three weeks. The amount greatly troubled me. I shrank from asking it, but was finally led, by a strange providence, to accept this fee.

What the "strange providence" was we are not told; only that God had shown in multitudinous ways the wisdom of the decision, that any loyal student would regard three hundred dollars as quite an inadequate equivalent for the instruction he had received, and that many indigent students had been trained for nothing.

Unfortunately the students were not always loyal. Some were so distinctly disloyal that it was necessary to sue them in the courts for their tuition fees. In others there was the hideous note of apostasy. There was George Tuttle, a stalwart young seaman who was "so surprised and frightened," when he cured a girl of dropsy by the employment of the revered Mother's methods that he washed his hands of Christian Science ever after. There was Wallace Wright, the bank accountant who, after a period of devout conformity, broke into violent revolt and challenged the revered Mother, since she denied the existence of matter, to raise the dead and to support herself without air and nourishment. There was young Richard Kennedy, the head of a small box factory, who, after helping Mrs. Glover Patterson to set up a mind clinic on the third floor of Miss Magoon's girls' school, could not be induced to give up his head-rubbing, was accused of cheating at cards, and sued in the courts on a promissory note. There was Lucretia Brown of Ipswich, a student who, at Mary Baker's instigation, brought an action against Daniel Spofford (also a student), alleging that Daniel Spofford had employed "malicious animal magnetism" against her and had caused her to have a serious relapse by the suggestion that she was ill. But perhaps worst of all there were the eight students who drew up a memorandum accusing the revered

Mother of bad temper, love of money, and "the appearance of hypocrisy." Such were the trials which beset the origins of the new apostolate.

Nevertheless, progress was made. Poor people came to the healer's door in search of relief from their pains and aches. Students paid fees and attended classes. Number 8 Broad Street, Lynn, an agreeable frame house, comfortable though not ambitious, with bow windows and balconies and a lawn and an outlook on the Lynn Common, was purchased (March 31st, 1875) for 5,650 dollars, a sum sufficient to indicate the beginnings of a substantial practice. The movement was proceeding by modest steps, but it was going forward all the same. It was in the little house at Lynn that the final touches were given to the literary work which had occupied Mary Baker for nine years. It was entitled *Science and Health*. The first edition, published in 1875 with the aid of a financial contribution from two students, was of a thousand copies.[1]

---

[1] In 1884 a *Key to the Scriptures* (in reality a fantastic interpretation of a few chapters of Genesis and a passage in the Apocalypse) was added to the volume, which was henceforth entitled *Science and Health with Key to the Scriptures.*

THE PROPHETESS

In the pleasant house at Lynn, life proceeded for a time without serious perturbations. More patients came to be cured of their ailments; more students enrolled themselves for lectures; and a little society was even formed pledged to contribute a sum of ten dollars weekly in order to enable special Sunday services to be held at which Mrs. Mary Baker Patterson would officiate as preacher. Everything, however, was still in a very small way. The students and patients were men and women of humble station, mostly from the shoe and boot factories of Lynn. The financial support available for the movement, though it had been materially increased, was still slight. The book, upon which so many hopes had been built, had failed to create a sensation. The craft of Christian Science was afloat upon the waters, but it was not yet out upon the open seas. Could nothing be done to accelerate advance? Many a drapery store, many a business in steel or hardware, had secured for itself a nationwide advertisement and a large holding in gilt-edged securities in a shorter time than had elapsed between the death of Dr. Quimby and the publication of *Science and Health.* Yet the causes retarding advance were obvious enough. The circle of men and women round Mrs. Glover were wholly devoid of business ability and experience. If the concern were to thrive, it was imperative to strengthen the direction without delay. The manner in which this was done provides a quaint episode in the history of modern religions. Mrs. Glover, as she now preferred to call herself, undeterred by her two unfortunate matrimonial experiences and divorced from Dr. Patterson, allowed herself to be led to the altar by a quiet and submissive business man.

One day a certain Mrs. Godfrey pricked her finger with a needle. The wound festered. A physician, with the folly to be expected of his tribe, advised amputation. Mrs. Godfrey declined to be amputated, visited some relations who were Mrs. Glover's patients, and was cured of her sore by the spiritual powers of Mrs. Glover.[1] Now Mrs. Godfrey had a bachelor friend in East Boston, who was in poor health. He is described as "a grave,

---

[1] I follow here, though, as always, with much hesitation, Miss Wilbur's pious guidance.

THE PROPHETESS 51

sweet-tempered man," who at this time was earning his livelihood as agent for a firm of sewing-machines. His name was Asa Gilbert Eddy. What could be more simple than that Mrs. Godfrey should introduce her gentle business friend to Mrs. Glover? What more inevitable than that Mrs. Glover should cure him? And what more suitable than that Mr. Eddy, cured and converted and well experienced in the whole business of handling and pushing the sale of goods, should be commanded to propose marriage to Mrs. Glover? The happy pair were united on New Year's Day, 1877, by a Unitarian clergyman. The marriage licence describes the bride as younger by sixteen years than her true age.

There was a peculiar circumstance which made a marriage to this safe, dull, obedient little man an urgent necessity to our heroine. Though God's mind was everywhere, there were nevertheless directed against God's prophetess enemy minds, malignant minds, minds practising animal magnetism, minds draining away the energies of the good, thwarting cures, stealing patients, inducing those disagreeable thoughts which mortal mind describes as illnesses, impeaching the true doctrine. There was the ex-pupil Kennedy, with his far too prosperous head-rubbing practice; there was the ex-pupil and "mesmeric outlaw" Spofford, always thinking of her injuriously, sapping her influence, practising without manipulation, resisting her written entreaties that he should *not* think of her. At this stage of her physical life these fears and suspicions became tormenting obsessions. Angry and harassed, assailed sometimes by violent fits of hysteria, at other times by a recurrence of that spinal irritation which Quimby had relieved but not wholly cured, she clutched at Asa G. Eddy as a prop and support against her foes.

Many years later, and long after he had been dead and buried, the following tribute was paid to the memory of this serviceable little man by the woman whose sudden choice has made him famous throughout the world. "Dr. Eddy," remarks his widow, "was the first student publicly to announce himself as a Christian Scientist, and place those symbolic words on his office sign. He forsook all to follow this line of light. He was the first organ-

THE PROPHETESS 53

iser of a Christian Science Sunday school, which he superintended. He also taught a special Bible class; and he lectured so ably on scriptural topics that clergymen of other denominations listened to him with deep interest. He was remarkably successful in mind-healing, and untiring in his chosen work."

All this is very well and becoming, but it fails to state the specific nature of Mr. Eddy's services to the movement. He helped his wife to tackle the whole question of the copyright of *Science and Health*. He saw to it that the second and third editions were properly launched and adequately protected; that the authoress obtained her royalties; that she was shielded against piracy; and that the sacred text was preserved from adulteration. These were important services. The finance of the movement was placed upon an unassailable foundation. Few business propositions in the book-selling world could be more attractive than a new Bible, coequal with, and supplementary to the old, and possessed of talismanic virtues, so that by the faithful study of its contents the possessor could preserve his health and be delivered from physical aches and pains without the knife of the surgeon or the phial of the doctor. For such a Bible it was wisely judged that the great American republic would pay three dollars.

There was another way in which Mr. Eddy proved his usefulness to the movement. He was a Boston man, with a circle of Boston acquaintances, and while his wife preached, lectured, and healed at Lynn, he opened a missionary movement in Boston. Then, in the summer of 1879, Mrs. Eddy began to lecture in the Athens of the United States. Here was a larger life, a great eagerness for novelties of all kinds, a wealthy clientèle of unoccupied persons in search of health, religion, or fashionable excitement. Here Mrs. Eddy, now the Reverend Mother, a graceful figure tastefully dressed in black silk, her chestnut hair not yet tinted against the advance of old age, her eyes of the deepest blue (or were they grey?), but shielded with spectacles since "she bore the vices of the world," her voice clear and musical, would lecture to large audiences. Always confident, always serene, always abounding in sonorous biblical phraseology, she created upon her listeners that impression of "poise" which in the sharp tingling New England air is so much valued as a sedative for jangled nerves and the uneasy conscience. Some of the best Boston families were drawn into the movement, the women leading and the men-folk following in their train.

Nevertheless, it must not be supposed that the reception of Mr. Eddy within the Holy of Holies was effected without acrimony or remonstrance. Old friends were discarded, old confidences undermined. The hopeless inefficiency of Mr. Spofford, who had so sadly mismanaged the business of marketing the first edition of Mrs. Eddy's Bible as to leave no profits for the authoress, was shown up. Defaulters were brought into court for failure to pay tuition fees. Along with many substantial accomplishments (such as the establishment of a Church in Boston, and a Metaphysical College, in 1881, "giving ample instruction in every scientific method of medicine"), there was a disagreeable atmosphere of jealousy, bitterness, and reprisals. A charge of conspiracy to murder was even brought against Mr. Eddy and a Christian Science student which could be traced back to the general feeling of disaffection caused by the recent changes of management. That this cuckoo should have found his way into the comfortable Christian Science nest and should have ejected many of the chicks was a thought which some established practitioners of mental healing found hard to bear. To the concentrated hatred of these malcontents Mrs. Eddy, whose mind was obsessed with the idea of malicious animal magnetism, ascribed the tragedy which has now to be recounted.

In the early summer of 1882 Mr. Eddy fell seriously ill. To the minds of the faithful there was something disturbing in the thought that the virtuous consort of the Holy Mother should take to a bed of sickness. Surely if ever there was an occasion in which prayer might be expected to exercise an efficacious operation, it was this! The patient was a faith-healer. His wife was the most illustrious of all faith-healers. If the application of Christian Science was unavailing to heal Mr. Eddy, what hopeful result could be expected from its operation where patient and healer were less firmly established in the faith, less pure in doctrine, less whole-hearted in their determination to conquer the evil thing? But Mr. Eddy did not respond to treatment. Then, in an access of human weakness, the devoted wife invoked medical aid. Dr. Rufus K. Noyes was a distinguished Boston physician. He diagnosed the illness as heart disease, and prescribed "rest and tonic, digitalis and strychnine." To the Reverend Mother the diagnosis and remedies were alike impermissible. Mr. Eddy was suffering from a suggestion of arsenical poison emanating from the ill-will of his enemies. There was nothing in the theory of heart disease, nothing in the tonics. The way to cure Mr. Eddy was to direct a strong counter-battery of prayer for his recovery against the formidable spiritual artillery which was being deployed against him. But if this was indeed the true diagnosis and this the true and only cure, why was it not efficacious? For the ordeal by prayer the Reverend Mother and her amiable consort were surely more than well matched against the inimical artificers of the murder conspiracy plot. Yet their efforts were unavailing. On July 3rd, 1882, Mr. Eddy expired. A post-mortem conducted by Dr. Noyes exhibited valvular trouble of the heart, but no arsenic poison or cancer. Mrs. Eddy was not convinced, but maintained, to the solace of the faithful, who were much perplexed by these untoward proceedings, that Mr. Eddy died of "mesmeric poison mentally administered." Since the poor man was refused the help of the tonics prescribed by the doctor, the Reverend Mother had no alternative but to meet the murmurs and doubts of the profane by showing a bold and consistent front. Who will pry into her heart as she watched the agonies of the dying man? Did she waver in her inflexible purpose? Did she feel that she might perhaps after all be wrong? Was it present to her mind that she might be losing a life to save a Church? If struggle there was, pride, faith, ambition gained a victory.

To the public her apology took the following form: "Circumstances debarred me from taking hold of my husband's case. He declared himself perfectly capable of carrying himself through, and I was so entirely absorbed in business that I permitted him to try, and when I awakened to the danger it was too late."

THE PROPHETESS 59

At sixty-one the Reverend Mother was no longer in the full vigour of youth. Her apostolate had been long and arduous. She had lost one husband by desertion and two by death. Her eccentricity had estranged her from her sisters; her masterful ways had affronted many of her disciples. A strong tincture of jealousy and distrust mingled in the circumambient atmosphere of docility and devotion. By some she was thought to be a charlatan, by others a dispenser of intellectual wares stolen from Quimby. The doctors, the mesmerists, the believers in the efficiency of animal magnetism, the spiritualists *pur sang,* were all against her. Even her hours of most intimate grief were not sacred from the profane. Public opinion condemned her to consent to the humiliating necessity of an autopsy upon her husband, and before his body was carried out to burial she was forced to give audience to the reporters and to assure them that her composure had been undisturbed in the supreme hour of bereavement. Yet nearly thirty years of life still lay before her, years of added achievement, of fruitful energy, and of widening influence. The death of Mr. Eddy seems neither to have abridged her reserves of nervous force nor lessened the sum of her physical powers. After a brief summer of rest in northern Vermont, she returned to the great business of extending the influence of her new religion. She added conquest to conquest and steadily gained in authority until she became one of the sacred institutions of America, the living centre of a prosperous creed, formed, defined, and developed by her persevering will, a quasimiraculous figure whose life, preserved to the extreme point of human longevity, was a standing rebuke to the scoffer and an incitement to salubrious living after the Christian rule.

When we ask what was the inner source of her power, the answer can only be that it was religion. Upon many of her intimates she made the impression of a saint. The great ideas of God, of immortality, of the soul, of a life penetrated by Christianity, were never far from her mind. Patients who came into her presence went away soothed and heartened by the spectacle of a nature so confident and composed and by so blithe an outlook on a dismal world. A woman in whom happiness was the fruit of faith, and faith, equally compounded

THE PROPHETESS 61

of a vision of other-worldliness and a strong sense of Divine dedication, was impervious to the ordinary ailments of mankind. Though she walked over thorns, her tread was as light as air. She lived on because the emotional stresses which come to men and women of divided aims or shrinking sensibilities did not appeal to her. The will to live, to work, to achieve her destiny, dominated all lesser promptings. Yet if there was in her that hard core of spiritual arrogance which is necessary to the propagation of a fighting faith, it was vested in a habit of appealing softness. The good bedside manner of the physician was united with the sustaining force of the missionary and the cool mensuration of a shrewd North American business head. Is it wonderful that the prophetess lived on? Can it be that she failed to recognise the enormous appeal of a message which found in the Christian life the sole positive condition of physical health, or that, recognising this, she failed to rejoice in its cash value? So the prophetess lived on till the verge of ninety, sustained inwardly by the illumination of faith, outwardly by accumulating tokens of material success, and regarded by her adoring circle as a wonderful survival from a vanished age.

The death of Mr. Eddy did not leave the Reverend Mother alone in the world. Her Bible, her lectures and sermons, her direction of the very lucrative Metaphysical College which she set up in her new Boston residence, brought her affluence and fame. How different was her case now from the situation in which she had been left when the volatile Dr. Patterson decamped with the daughter of the wealthy patient fifteen years before! Then she was needy, solitary, obscure. Now a circle of friends and disciples, many of them well furnished with the goods of this world and some of them financially interested in the success of her venture, stood round her, offering business counsels, ministering to her needs and comforts, a shield against the rude blasts of hostile criticism. Did she require a summer holiday retreat? There was the convenient Mr. Buswell, well to do, *bienpensant,* with a pleasant country house in North Vermont, very much at Mrs. Eddy's service. Did she need a secretary and business *factotum?* Mr. Calvin A. Frye, a childless bachelor of

THE PROPHETESS 63

twenty-eight, his worldly credentials duly sifted by Mr. Eddy, his religious orthodoxy unassailable (the son of a Christianly healed mother, himself a student of Christian healing at Lynn and a Christian healer in his native town of Lawrence), was ready to assume the rôle for an adequate pecuniary compensation. Mr. Frye was a treasure. To the end he remained the amanuensis, the steward, the guardian angel of the sacred purse.

By this time the Holy Mother's operations were beginning to assume a nation-wide and even an international scale. The Metaphysical College (founded in 1881) attracted students from Europe as well as from every part of the United States. Emissaries were dispatched to New York, to Chicago, to Cincinnati, and to other crowded centres of population to spread the good news. Apart from the public lectures in Boston, and the weekly Church services, a National Christian Scientist Association was formed, which held its first meeting in New York in 1886, advertising the fact that Christian Science was no longer a phenomenon confined to New England, but that congregations of the new faith were spread throughout the

Union. Moreover, in 1883 the prophetess decided that the hour had struck for invoking the resources of the Press. A monthly magazine, the *Christian Science Journal,* "an Independent Family Paper to promote health and morals," was launched upon a long and successful career.[1]

How could one elderly woman cope with the growing complexity and range of these operations? How check the dissidence of dissent, how curb the luxuriance of superstition, as the circle of the faithful grew ever wider and the personal energies of the Founder were slowly sapped by the remorseless passage of time? There are some religious movements which are singularly exempt from external shocks. They live by the inner light of spiritual natures, and do not affront the interests of a profession or the moral susceptibilities of the wise and good. Christian Science was not such a movement. When a woman died in childbed because Christian Science kept the doctor from the house, the profane murmured

[1] The Dentists were quick to perceive the professional value of a system calculated to allay the pains of their patients. Hence the dentists' advertisements in the early numbers of the journal. See especially C.S.J. Nov. 6th, 1884.

that a mother and her baby had been murdered by the zealots of a craze. One such case was even brought into court—a case in which a mother who was a professed healer sacrificed her own daughter and grandchild to the rigours of Christian Science, logic, a case in which Mrs Eddy herself was subpœnaed for the defence. Such disagreeable incidents called for great watchfulness in supervision and a careful husbandry of directing power.

The Reverend Mother was equal to these emergencies. She organised her household, redistributed her energies, wound up concerns which appeared to be running at a spiritual loss or likely to lead to trouble, and struck hard when occasion demanded. Finding that the original Christian Science Church was getting out of hand for lack of her personal supervision, she promptly closed it, dissolved the congregation, and wound up its affairs. Her will was law. "No sooner were my views made known than the proper measures were adopted to carry them out, the votes passing without a dissenting voice."

The Metaphysical College was brought to an abrupt end by an equal exercise of autocratic power, and for similar reasons. The Reverend Mother, "Professor of Obstetrics, Metaphysics, and Christian Science," found herself no longer equal to the great exertion of conducting classes. Popular and lucrative though the college might be, hard as it might be to forgo its tuition fees and its diploma fees, it was the part of prudence to bring its existence to a close. Without the shepherd to guide and even to correct, what would become of the sheep? A centre of orthodoxy might develop into a cradle of heresies. Yet to close an establishment at a time when it was fuller than ever of students was a step which demanded, if not a certain measure of courage, at least an official explanation. The Reverend Mother was not the woman to quail before such a call. She informed the world that she dreaded the "unprecedented popularity" of her college, that there was a danger in "being placed on earthly pinnacles," and that in order to refresh the spiritual life of the Church it was necessary to abate its earthly pride. "The time has come," announced the Directors of the College Board (October 29th, 1889), "wherein the great need is for more of the spirit instead

THE PROPHETESS 67

of the letter, and *Science and Health* is adapted to work this result." The language of the directors is not elegant, but their meaning is plain. *Science and Health* at three dollars a copy is a safer prophylactic against error than a college diploma. The prophetess too had come to the conclusion that too much learning was a dangerous thing.

"A Primary Class student," she observes, "richly imbued with the spirit of Christ, is a better healer and teacher than a Normal Class student who partakes less of God's love. After having received instruction in a Primary Class from me, or a loyal student, and afterwards studied thoroughly *Science and Health,* a student can enter upon the gospel work of teaching Christian Science, and so fulfil the command of Christ. But before entering this field of labour he must have studied the latest editions of my works, be a good Bible scholar and a consecrated Christian."

"He must have studied the latest editions of my works." What publisher could dream of a finer advertisement? The latest editions declared by their author to be an essential condition of Christian Science teaching! In proportion as her energies declined the authoress was disposed to attach an increasing measure of confidence to the healing powers of the book, the latest editions of which were still sustained at the remunerative price of three dollars.

It is a property of religious emotion to appeal at once to the noblest and to the basest of mankind. The Christian Science Movement is no exception to this rule. If some fine natures were attracted by the new teaching, they were greatly outnumbered by the unstable, the self-centred, the neurasthenic, and the ignorant, who discovered in the new creed something which might quiet the nerves, cheer the heart, and mystify the mind. An imaginary illness can only be helped by an imaginary cure, and in the cities of North America, where imaginary illnesses are endemic, the provision of imaginary cures assumes the magnitude of a public interest. The contrast between the hopefulness of the new doctrine and the dark and forbidding beliefs of popular Calvinism was an added recommendation. In the religious atmosphere of Protestant North America during the later half of the nineteenth century, the intelligence that God was benevolent, that cheerfulness was a duty, that illness and sin and death were unreal,

THE PROPHETESS 69

that immortality was guaranteed, but, above all, that a holy woman had discovered a new, certain, and inexpensive mode of easing pain and prolonging human life seemed like a message direct from heaven. Of the three great human interests, love, health, religion, two appeared to be promoted to an immeasurable degree by the new discovery. In general, people believe what they desire to believe. Philosophers may tell us that belief should be proportionate to evidence, and to minds trained in the logic of the sciences beliefs may be so reached and so graded, but the ordinary mind of the ordinary man and woman is only to a slight degree affected by the rules of evidence prescribed by the logician or observed by the judge. The ordinary person finds what he expects and expects what he desires. The student who had paid three hundred dollars for a course of Christian Science teaching was predisposed to the opinion that his money would not be thrown away. Once inscribed on the bead roll of Mrs. Eddy's pupils he was more than half converted to her doctrine. Still greater was the mesmeric influence exerted upon crowds, who had been led to expect, by all the arts of prefatory advertisement, great healing results from the presence of the holy lady. When the "Boston prophetess," as she was described by the advance agents of the creed, came to Chicago in June 1889 for the Spiritual Jubilee of the National Christian Science Association, the emotion of the audience was indescribable. Long before Mrs. Eddy appeared upon the platform, the hall was thronged with devotees who had been worked up into a glow of frenzied enthusiasm. An extempore speech of which no exact record remains, the reporters being too far overcome with emotion to take notes, was followed by a wild rush for the platform and an indescribable scene of confusion, everybody desiring to kiss the dress of the prophetess or to touch her hand, or to claim her healing help, or to express gratitude for some past cure. At a hotel reception on the following day, the same scene of almost riotous confusion was enacted, and dresses were torn and jewels lost as the excited guests hustled forward to salute the supreme healer. The chronicler is reminded of those distant days in the seventeenth century when a scro-

THE PROPHETESS 71

fulous and ragged crowd, rendered credulous by misery, would press round Charles II to be touched for the "king's evil."

These tumultuous compliments were little to the taste of the Reverend Mother, who was too wise a woman to encourage the follies of apotheosis and was now of an age when prudence and inclination alike combine to commend a life of comparative retirement. So the handsome residence in Commonwealth Avenue, with its twenty rooms and its views over the Charles River, was exchanged in the spring of 1889 for a house in Concord, and this again four years later for a roomy country home, standing in its own grounds and commanding a distant prospect of Bow and of the fields and hills connected with her childish days. Here, at Pleasant View, for such was the name of her villa, the Queen of Christian Science held her court for some fifteen quiet and happy years. Here, with the assistance of Mr. Frye and Mrs. Sargant, she would deal with her large correspondence, and for some years receive communicants flocking in from every part of the country. It was from Pleasant View that she put out the volume of *Mis-*

cellaneous Writings which forms part of the sacred canon; it was from this quiet retreat that she dissolved the Christian Church at Boston and directed the construction of that vast edifice of marble and granite whose dome dominates Boston City as the dome of St. Peter's, viewed from the Campagna, appears to roof in the whole city of Rome.

In the accomplishment of these tasks she was now assisted by many able business lieutenants, but we are asked to believe that hers was still the supreme directing mind. Her tastes were simple, her life ordered on a methodical plan. In summer she would rise at six, in winter before seven. In every day three hours were set apart for prayer and meditation. In the morning she would review her household, stroll in the garden, and work at her desk. After the midday dinner she would drive abroad in a brougham drawn by two black horses; and then only, save on the rare occasions of a visit to Boston, was she visible to the profane eye.

It would seem that she was exempt from that desiccation of the affections which often comes with advancing age. She had a pleasant

THE PROPHETESS

smile for children. In 1879 she attempted to interest her son in the mysteries of Christian Science, but the seed fell on stony ground, and George Glover, returning to the congenial West, ceased to be a possible prop and companion to his mother. His place was taken by a young doctor, whose compliance with the new faith was soon placed beyond suspicion. Dr. Forster was adopted as a son, made to add the name of Eddy to his own, and entrusted with responsible positions in the business hierarchy of the Church. Yet family affections, however genuine, were never allowed to overmaster the interests of the Cause. For her graceless son Mrs. Eddy made a provision of 245,000 dollars, and Dr. Forster Eddy was the recipient of a liberal, though less munificent, endowment; but gifts and legacies to individuals absorbed but a small part of the handsome fortune which the preaching and practice of the new religion had brought to its happy patentee. The greater portion of Mrs. Eddy's considerable estate was vested in the hands of trustees for the endowment of the Mother Church and the promotion of the true doctrine.

It was the fate of this singular lady on more than one occasion to extricate herself with little or no loss of authority from circumstances of great humiliation. In extreme old age Mrs. Eddy's sanity was challenged in a legal action by the jealous rapacity of a son, a stepson, and a nephew. The story of a wealthy old lady, captured by a gang of alien and sycophantic fortune-hunters, and kept apart from her nearest of kin lest they should obtain a share of the inheritance, is familiar to the comic stage. It was not unnatural that the Glovers and Bakers should view with some feelings of irritation the thick zariba of secretaries and lady helpers who beset the approaches to the saintly lady of fortune; but the plea of insanity could not be sustained. After a year of legal agitations—for in Massachusetts the chariot of Justice moves at a deliberate pace—the alert intelligence of the aged prophetess routed her assailants. Having made a fortune by her wits, Mrs. Eddy proposed to spend it in her own way.

Indeed, the last few years of her life were in some respects the most remarkable, for they were characterised by important developments in the growth of the new religion—the revision of the canon, the enlargement and completion of the Mother Church in Boston, and the foundation of that great and well-informed daily newspaper, which, under the title of the *Christian Science Monitor,* circulates throughout the world. It was chiefly in order to further this last project that Mrs. Eddy, at the age of eighty-seven, was impelled to give up her pleasant country house on the outskirts of Concord and to settle down in the suburbs of Boston. Here, at Chestnut Hill, installed in a luxurious mansion, with a little army of clerks, secretaries, and helpers at her beck and call, the venerable autocrat was in a position to supervise the rising fabric of a great publishing house and the growing activities of a sumptuous Church. All things prospered. The plants of journalism—sown, watered, and tended for so many years—burst out into sudden and overwhelming luxuriance. A daily newspaper was decreed, christened, and issued to a receptive public, its first number adorned by an editorial from the indefatigable pen of the lady director, then in her eighty-eighth year. "The object of the

Monitor is," she wrote, "to injure no man and to bless all the world." A clean paper, free of base and degraded appeals, cheerful and well informed, was her last practical contribution to social welfare.

To the end she observed those habits of personal neatness which naturally belong to the business woman who, in forty years of Church leadership, had never, as she was wont to observe, made a single mistake. Her hands were carefully manicured, her hair scrupulously disposed, her dress very costly, well cut, and drawn from a large and various wardrobe. A diamond marquise ring and a handsome diamond cross evidenced the lady of property. In the large household at Chestnut Hall everyone was her obedient servant. The meals were punctual to a minute, the discipline vigilant and severe, the diurnal routine of a monastic precision. Yet the Mother's soul was not at rest amid these circumstances of established pomp and authority, these flattering evidences of her great achievement. Apprehensions of enemy minds, enemy influences working against her, and only to be kept at

THE PROPHETESS

bay by constant vigilance, could not be suppressed. The thought of death, possibly sudden, possibly coming in the night assailed her. It was the kind of underhand stroke which the malignant magnetism of her enemies would contrive. "There is a new form of sin and malpractice," she observed to a faithful attendant, "that has been revealed to me, and that no one has ever discovered before, and that is that evil is trying to produce sudden death in sleep." How were these hateful dangers to be repelled? Only by a bodyguard of loyal healers, men and women of the best physique, unlikely to give scandal by illness and death, and available to supply "adverse treatment" against the enemy. So healers were recruited in suitable numbers, and the night was divided into four watches, and to each watcher was given the password for the night indicating the foe. To Mrs. Sargant was specially assigned the duty of "watching the weather and bringing it into accord with normal conditions," for the Holy Mother objected to snow and thunder. "Make a law that there should be no snow this season" was her order to the watch on June 15th, 1910.

If snow was bad, thunder was worse. Yet had not the Holy Mother often dissipated a thunderstorm by merely looking at it? The serviceable Mrs. Sargant was told off to send the thunder to the right about.

Enough of the eccentricities of extreme old age. Her secretaries, as became the servants of a spirit so keen and vigorous, were competent to the end. One December day in 1910, as she came in from her afternoon drive, chilled, old, and weary, a tablet was brought to her, upon which she wrote in pencil the words "God is my life." That was her last message to the world. A few days after she was dead of pneumonia. Six hundred and sixty-eight churches in the United States acknowledged in her their spiritual chief.

It is vain to represent a great woman of affairs as a sweet, sentimental figure. In this rough world sweetness and sentiment do not build organizations and amass fortunes. Florence Nightingale, a far nobler figure than Mrs. Eddy, was not altogether the amiable, tender creature of the Victorian legend, but, as Jowett once described her, "very violent";

THE PROPHETESS

and equally violent and compelling was the will of the woman who founded the Christian Science Church. The image of a saintly healer, gentle, compassionate, penetrated with mystical devotion, thinking always of others, never of herself, and winning her way to influence by the magic of eloquence and virtue, is as far from the reality as are the photographs which give to Mrs. Eddy the appearance of a finished lady of society. The Founder of Christian Science did not look like a fashion plate. There was power in her well-shaped head, there were storm-clouds in her deep-set, shrewd, uneasy, eyes, there was irritability and ill-temper in her thin and sensitive lips, character in her domineering nose. Mrs. Eddy was ill to live with. She was not a woman to accept atmosphere from others. Wherever she went she brought her own uncanny climate with her. Whether as a wife or as a prophet, or as a self-invited guest, she exacted much and conceded nothing. Like Florence Nightingale she would have her way.

What the true physical interpretation of her life may be, let the expert determine. For more than forty years she was nervous, ailing, self-absorbed, without an object upon which to expend her remarkable store of nervous energy, consuming herself in little verses, little articles, and in one tiresome effort after another to capture the health which would never come. Then she met Quimby, the mind-healer. At once she experienced a complete change of outlook. From Quimby she obtained an assurance of health, of usefulness, of importance for the world. In Quimby's teaching she found the key to a new and animating gospel, in the light of which all human values experienced an exciting change. She resolved to preach the new evangel—first of all as a disciple; then, after the death of the master, by a peculiar process of self-deception, as its veritable and only creator. By degrees her latent powers of business organisation reveal themselves. She sees how money matters, and how it is to be made. She founds a college, a church, a world organisation, newspapers. She writes the Bible of the New Faith, and, by every art and device known to the ambitious ecclesiastic, the pushing publisher, the advertiser of medical wares, secures for it a wide and lucrative circulation. She is swift to see where money may run out of the church, and to stop up the holes; prompt in the suppression of heresies, and fierce in their denunciation. Free preaching, free writing, free learning are proscribed. The book, the very profitable book, is the sole deposit of the true doctrine, as its author is the sole and untrammelled exponent of the Church in all its branches and workings. "Never admit anything which may weigh against ourselves," said the worldly wise woman to Mr. Dickey at the end of her long career. It was a maxim characteristic of the superb confidence which made of her the most successful business boss whose brains have been employed in the exploitation of a creed.

II

THE CREED

A covert place
Where you might think to find a din
Of doubtful talk, and a live flame
Wandering, and many a shape whose name
Not itself knoweth, and old dew,
And your own footsteps meeting you,
And all things going as they came.
—Rossetti.

Can a person be treated metaphysically for an excess of fat?

Yes. —*Christian Science Journal,* November, 1884.

THE CREED

SOME of the greatest books of the world are among the shortest. That so few words should have meant so much to the human race is part of the miracle of Plato's *Apology,* of St. Mark's Gospel, of the *Contrât Social.* The Bible of the Christian Science religion has none of this immortal velocity. It is inordinately, miraculously long. Of arrangement and orderly progress there is not a vestige. There is no reason why the first chapter should not be the last, or the last the first. There is generally no reason why one sentence should follow and not precede another. The English is cumbersome and uncultivated. There is no sense of logic, no capacity for the development of an argument, no humour, no wit, no eloquence, no poetry, none of the recognised ornaments and graces of style. But if these things are absent, no one can refuse to *Science and Health, with Key to the Scriptures,* the tribute which belongs to sheer bulk. "If that idea is a good one and true," Quimby would remark, "it will do no harm to have it in two or more times." The disciple acted on the master's maxim. Her wealth of repetition is such that it cannot fail to extort from the attentive reader a sentiment of bewildered and fatigued respect. Without this crowning demonstration it would not have been thought possible to expend so many words upon a theme which St. Paul would have made intelligible in a chapter or Voltaire in a page.

The philosophy of Mrs. Eddy is a simple, uncompromising idealism. It is summarised in three fundamental axioms.

> God is all in all
> God is good, good is mind
> God spirit being all, nothing is matter—

propositions which, as the authoress observes, may be equally well understood if they are read backward, which mathematically proves their exact correspondence with truth!

Now the theory that everything is a thought in the mind of God has been held by many a first-class intellect. It presents certain obvious difficulties, which it is the business of the philosopher to meet and overcome, if his hypothesis is to be made acceptable to the reader's mind. But a theory of this kind is capable of being exhibited as an explanation of knowledge and as an interpretation of experience, with a given expenditure of dialectical skill. Moreover, if a thinker chooses to take up his stand upon the platform of absolute idealism, if he chooses to say that there is nothing in the world but the spirit of God, and consequently that everything which lives and moves and has its being may be most properly described as "moments in the process of the Divine reason," there is no means of refuting him, unless, indeed, he shrinks from carrying his premise to a logical conclusion. The philosopher cannot begin by saying that everything is God's spirit, and then proceed to make exceptions. He cannot on the ground of some assumed moral incompatibility draw the line at medicines, or surgical instruments, or doctors. He cannot say that human pleasure is part of the Divine mind, but that human pain is not; that the phenomenon which we describe as health has a place in the thought of God, but that the phenomenon which we describe as illness has no such place; that the experience known as life is part of the world spirit, but that the experience known as death is foreign to it. In a word, he cannot be a monist and a dualist at one and the same time.

Now, in general, it is not Mrs. Eddy's practice to argue at all. She prefers to lay down the law; but on the rare occasions when she exchanges incantation for argument, her method is remarkable. Her favourite premise seems to be that two things, which are opposite to one another, cannot co-exist. "If God is good, is real, then evil, the opposite of God, is unreal." It is a principle which carries us far. If life is real, then death is unreal. If pleasure is real, then pain is unreal. "Life, God, omnipotence, good, deny death, evil, sin, disease." By the same sweeping principles it would seem that white should deny black, that man should deny woman, and that, if day be real, night is nothing but a dream.

Nevertheless, this is the core of Mrs. Eddy's

THE CREED

doctrine. Spirit is everything, matter is nothing. "Spirit never requires matter to aid it, or through which to act." Sin, death, disease, pain, are the illusions of mortal mind. Contrary to universal belief, they have no real existence. When a man says, "I have a pain in my right arm" he is not expressing the truth. The right arm, which is matter, cannot feel. The pain is merely a false belief. Work on the belief, diminish it, extirpate it, and the pain is gone. The belief, the feeling, have no connection with anything material. Fear, hygiene, physiology, medicine, these are the causes of the false beliefs, which are miscalled illnesses. How could men, made, as the Scriptures aver, in God's image, be created dyspeptic? God is not dyspeptic. Dyspepsia, therefore, does not come from God, is no thought in the Divine intelligence, but a false belief of mortal mind, the child of fear.

As disease is a false belief, so also is infection a false belief. Cholera, typhoid, mumps, chicken-pox are false beliefs propagated by fear, destroyed by courage. An isolation hospital encourages the evil which it attempts to arrest. "Obesity is an adipose belief in yourself as a substance." The diseases of animals are accounted for by the theory that they have been corrupted by the beliefs of men. A consistent Christian Scientist will not, therefore, call in a veterinary surgeon to a cow suffering from pneumonia, but will endeavour to cure himself and his friends of their erroneous belief in the reality of pneumonia among cows.

Some obvious criticisms at once occur to the profane. If matter is unreal, why eat and drink? If disease is a false belief, why does a man who unconsciously swallows a lethal poison die? If everything is Mind, what is a dollar and for what reason is it pursued?

Mrs. Eddy's reply to these and similar objections is very characteristic. "We learn," she says, "in science food neither helps nor harms man." We certainly do not learn this interesting fact from experience, but it is, of course, a logical deduction from Mrs. Eddy's first principle. But if the taking of food and drink is quite indifferent, why should the human race be put to the intolerable cost and labour of providing itself with these indifferent nonentities? Once admit the premise that

THE CREED

matter is unreal, we are bound to accept the conclusion that food and drink are negligible. The Founder of Christian Science shrinks from this absurdity. "To stop utterly eating and drinking until your belief changes in regard to these things were error." Did Mrs. Eddy herself ever change her belief with regard to these things? Never. Her meals were punctually served and regularly consumed. *Noblesse oblige.* She should have given an example to her followers of the immaterial life.

If it is an error to stop eating and drinking until one's belief changes with respect to the necessity of food and drink, it is safe to say that the human race will never stop eating and drinking. But why limit this concession to food and drink? Why is it not equally an error to act against a not less clear conviction that anæsthetics and medicine are sometimes necessary, that diseases may be infectious or contagious, or that poison kills? To such questions the Founder of Christian Science vouchsafes no answer.

One peculiar feature of Mrs. Eddy's doctrine is that illness is not only induced and fostered by the false beliefs of the invalid, but by the false beliefs of the rest of the world. Even if a man is not aware of his illness, and has therefore no false belief, he is liable to suffer for the false belief or morbid mind of other people. If a child be murdered by a lethal dose of arsenic infused into a pudding, the arsenic is not a poison; what kills is the false belief of a large number of people that arsenic has deleterious effects. Abolish that belief, and the consumption of arsenic in indefinite quantities will be innocuous.

That matter cannot co-operate with spirit is one of the cardinal axioms of *Science and Health*. It appears, however, that there are exceptions even to universal truths. The malpractitioner does not vainly manipulate the head of his patient. There is virtue—or, rather, vice—in his manipulation. "Manipulating the head, we discovered, establishes between patient and practitioner a mental communication not in the least understood by the patients or the people. Through this medium the doctor holds more direct influence over their minds than the united forces of

THE CREED

education and public sentiment." It might have been expected that the discovery of spiritual evils so formidable and so malign flowing from the purely physical process of head-rubbing might have impelled the metaphysician to reconsider her premises. Not in the least. The sinister control of the head-rubber—"a sort of popery that takes away voluntary action"—is accepted as entirely compatible with the conviction that heads are unreal.

A theory of the universe which ignores the greater part of human experience is no theory at all. Had Mrs. Eddy contented herself with saying that spiritual life is the ultimate basis of reality, or that all happenings are to the percipient facts of consciousness, she would have stood within the bounds of philosophical sanity; but she went much further; she declared that to be illusion within which the major part of the human race find their only reality. She not only denies reality of any kind to all those human experiences, however they may be interpreted by metaphysicians, out of which the mind has built up its conception of reality, but she makes no attempt to relate these experiences in any way to reality. The body is declared to be unreal; the human mind, thinking its ordinary thoughts, is unreal; the whole visible universe is an illusion. It is never explained how these unrealities become present to consciousness, when they arose, or how they are related—if, indeed, they stand in any relation—to the one acknowledged reality. The true nature of the problem of knowledge is not even dimly apprehended.

The theological implications of this fantastic scheme of idealism are not as clearly apprehended by the votaries of Christian Science as they deserve to be. God is spirit, and there is nothing real but spirit. There is no such thing in Mrs. Eddy's philosophy as personality, no such thing as that which, in the words of an eminent modern thinker,[1] has been truly described as "the most real of all reals, the latest and fullest expression of the supreme reality, which gives reality to all other reals." Personality which is not only mental and spiritual, but also organic and material, the personality which we know more intimately

[1] J. C. Smuts, *Holism and Evolution*.

THE CREED

than anything else, and through which alone we can know anything else, is dissolved into nothingness by this philosophy. We cannot imagine the body of a living human being to exist without a mind, or the mind of a living human being to exist without a body. How mind acts on body, or body on mind, are questions of the utmost complexity, but that there is an intimate action and reaction between these two sides of human personality, only to be distinguished one from another by a process of intellectual abstraction, is one of the most familiar facts of observation. Mrs. Eddy, however, will have nothing to say to flesh and blood. For her the body is nonexistent. There is in man a disembodied spirit which is real, which is, indeed, the only real; and apart from this there is "mortal mind," which is unreal, though how mortal mind can be at all if it be unreal, is nowhere explained. The conception of personality, then, as the highest category of being is alien to Mrs. Eddy's philosophy. She does not recognise personality in the full sense to man; she denies it altogether to God. That the Universal realises itself through individual bodies, and in particular things; that spirit and matter are both interdependent aspects of reality—these truths do not occur to her. With a large gesture of contempt she sweeps the cosmos, so far as it is apprehended by the human senses, into the dim and shadowy limbo of the unreal.

Wild and visionary as this one-sided idealism may appear to be, it carries with it an unfortunate practical consequence. Mrs. Eddy was driven by her principles to a belief in witchcraft. If a good mind acting upon another mind is sufficient to create health, an evil mind so acting may, by parity of reasoning, produce illness. The Christian Scientist is bound by principle to believe in absent treatment. He is bound to believe that the spirit is not impeded in its operation by the accident of distance. If the healer can cure a patient at a yard's distance by mental treatment, he can equally cure him at a distance of a thousand miles. The consequences are formidable. Not all minds are good. Not all minds are informed by the principles of Christian Science. There are evil, malignant minds, willing arsenic into the intestines of their enemies (such was the *spécialité* of the student

Arens), and contriving mischief in every direction. "False beliefs," or, as ordinary mortals are wont to term them, diseases, are generally caused by these demoniacal minds. Thus her own bout of ill-health in 1877 was undoubtedly due to Kennedy, "the Nero of to-day, regaling himself through a mental method with the tortures of individuals"— Kennedy, her early partner in the healing business, whom she had accused of cheating at cards, and who now, in revenge, used mesmeric influence against her.

How were these demonic influences to be met and parried? One way was by adverse treatment. A number of pure, good minds could be directed to think against the evil mind. Thus Spofford was submitted to twenty-five hours of adverse treatment, administered by relays of the faithful, organised under the direction of the Reverend Mother herself. But it was difficult to be armed against all antagonists; difficult to adjust the antidote to the bane. Mental malpractice would sometimes reach such a pitch as to make a place almost uninhabitable, or an individual quite unbearable. Boston was full of malpractice. As for

Mrs. Hopkins, "You are so full of mesmerism," observed Mrs. Eddy to that lady, "that your eyes stick out like boiled codfish's." A fierce chapter of demonology, in which the Reverend Mother gave full vent to her personal dislikes, was included in some early editions of *Science and Health,* but afterwards wisely omitted from subsequent issues of the book.

Let it not, however, be imagined that this dark aspect of the philosophy of the Christian Scientist vanished with the fourth edition of *Science and Health.* The fear of mental malpractice dominated Mrs. Eddy throughout her life, and is stamped upon the liturgical manual which is still employed in Christian Science Churches. There are many who are attracted by a religion which announces the unreality of pain and sin, which uproots fear, and proclaims the sovereign virtues of courage. But the careful student of *Science and Health* has no great cause for joyfulness. The shining medal has an obverse, darkly stained with gloom and suspicion. Everywhere, and all the time, impalpable spiritual influences are working, evil and wicked thoughts pro-

THE CREED

ceed from wicked minds, inducing pains, illness, death, foiling the efforts of Christian healers, and impeding the triumph of the true faith.

The doctrine of mind-cure, so far from being peculiar to Mrs. Eddy, has always, and in every generation, entered as an element into the wisdom of the wise. In the later half of the nineteenth century the subject of psychotherapy, or mind-healing, began to attract the special attention of doctors and psychologists on both sides of the Atlantic. A large literature sprang up upon nervous ailments and mental cures. Men of intellectual eminence in all the principal European countries recognised that it was a field of investigation, part medical, part psychological, from which, though little attention had hitherto been paid to it, a rich harvest of remedial knowledge might be reaped. The microscope of science was brought to bear upon the phenomena of hypnotism, of moralising cures, and even of religious miracles, such as those which are reported from Lourdes. The rival schools of Nancy and of the Salpêtrière shot into fame, and in the 'eighties the strange performances of the hysterical patients of the wonder-working Charcot supplied a favourite theme of conversation to the wits of Paris.

America is a land of popular enthusiasms. In the eastern states of the American Republic the theory of the mind-cure, passing from the consulting-room or the laboratory into the street, developed into a cult and a rule of life, pursued with single-minded and uncritical fervour by thousands to whom the names of Charcot and Liebault, of Braid and Forel, were utterly unknown. In the prevailing optimism of an adventurous society, snatching at every novelty, and swiftly advancing in material wealth, there was something specially attractive in a religion of simple healthy-mindedness. It was a welcome contrast to the melancholy and forbidding tradition of Puritan austerity to learn that happiness was the key to health, and that health was the first article in the code of duty. The idea that it was in every one's power, by a courageous exercise of will and intelligence, if not wholly to overcome, at least greatly to attenuate, the evils of the flesh, flattered the pride and sustained the hopes of a sanguine and self-confident community. "He was not," remarks Mrs. Eddy of one of her converts, "satisfied with a manlike God, but wanted to become a Godlike man"; and on the assumption that pain, illness, and sin are non-existent, or may be properly and safely left unnoticed, the aspiration of Mrs. Eddy's convert was not fantastic. A spirit of optimism was in the air. It was nourished by the prose of Emerson and the verse of Walt Whitman, by the doctrine of evolution, by the advance of the country in material wealth, and by the evidence to be found in the four Gospels of the affinity of man with the Divine Nature. Above all, there was in the leaders of the mind-cure movement, says William James, "an instinctive belief in the all-saving power of healthy activities as such, in the conquering efficiency of courage, hope, and trust, and a correlative contempt for doubt, fear, worry, and all the nervous precautionary states of mind." In fine, however much the apostles of the new mental hygiene may have differed in their ultimate metaphysical beliefs, they were agreed in thinking that pessimism led to weakness and optimism to power.

In all these doctrines there is a solid core of incontestable truth and good sense. Many people persuade themselves into illness. Many contract mental habits which tend to lower their vitality and resisting-power when illness comes. The twin demons of worry and ill-temper are always on the watch, and, unless they be combated with vigour, soon establish a fatal ascendancy. A life filled with hygienic anxieties, a life in which drugs, doctors, and diet are allowed to become a predominant interest, is unlikely to be either happy or long. Good spirits are often the precedent condition of good health, and good spirits need nourishment.

The spiritual medicament appropriate to each particular case may vary. Some require rest and solitude, others travel and change of scene; some a simplification of life, others a multiplication and heightening of vital interests. To some the wise physician of the soul will prescribe the regular sedative of religious exercises, of the repetition of some optimistic incantation, such as, "Every day and in every way I grow better and better." The indulgence in reflections and experiences calculated to depress the spirits, such as complaints of the weather, attendance at funerals, or unavailing regrets, receives the censure of these hierophants of hygiene. To some patients the processes of psycho-analysis or confession are said to bring relief. The skilled psychologist disperses a suppressed complex of painful emotions by a process of artful cross-examination, and restores the mind to healthy elasticity. The moralising bedside talk of M. Dubois of Berne, who lays before his patients the ideal of an active and courageous life; the psycho-analytical methods of the disciples of Dr. Freud, who attempt to relieve the sick mind of its secret burden; the Emmanuel Church Health Class at Boston, which lays stress on weekly religious services, the hygienic value of hymns and prayers, of an optimistic temper, and a day filled with a variety of interests—these modes of treatment show the increasing importance which public opinion had begun to attach to the mind-cure of an element in healing in the later half of the nineteenth century.

The idea of calling in the mind to help to cure the ailments of the body was so simple, it was suggested by so much that was the common experience of mankind, and, once apprehended, was capable of being applied in so many ways by persons entirely devoid of scientific knowledge, that Mrs. Eddy's achievement in creating for her own particular form of the mind-cure doctrine the dignity of an institutional religion is extraordinary. The odds against her success in this courageous enterprise were formidable. All that was really true and helpful in her system could be taught by those who were not members of the Church or believers in its philosophy. All that was peculiar or paradoxical was open to criticism or ridicule. From the first the Founder of Christian Science was encompassed by rivals, and by rivals of the most dangerous kind— by mesmerists, spiritualists, apostles of the New Thought, rebellious pupils; by rivals, that is to say, who were directly competing with her in her own market, selling their mind-cures in competition with her mind-cures, matching her miracles by their miracles, and making the same type of appeal to the same common human cravings for some short cut to health, happiness, and longevity. Yet this obscure woman overcame all her rivals, formulated her religion, patented it, surrounded it with a spiritual and legal palisade, and, after making it a paying concern, died in extreme old age, opulent, honoured and victorious. Why was this? Why, of all the many modes of mind-cure which had a vogue in the United States, did Christian Science alone achieve the dignity of an established and popular religion?

The name counted for much. In two words it combined the deepest spiritual interests of the American people, Christianity and science. The doctrine of Mrs. Eddy was certainly not Christian in the accepted sense of that word; still less was it scientific; but the title was a stroke of genius. That it was first employed by Quimby in a casual, unsystematic way does not detract from the credit of his pupil. Mrs. Eddy was the first to see the supreme value of those two words Christian Science as the trademark of her great exclusive venture. With fine business instinct she seized upon that happy title and made it her own. In the United States, where the psychology of advertisement is a serious subject of academic study, there is no better or more impudent commercial label in any line of goods.

The title was the more attractive because it implied that the venerable but still popular fabric of the Christian religion was now to receive from the capable hands of an American lady improvements and additions which were long overdue. "The age is reaching out," observed the Reverend Mother, "to the perfect Principle of things; is pushing towards perfection in art, invention, and manufactures. Why then should religion be stereotyped, and we obtain [*sic*] a more perfect and practical Christianity?" That was a question which found an echo in many an honest Yankee heart. A Christianity more perfect and practical! A Christianity of good cheer, rid of the Devil and hell fire! A Christianity which could heal you of any disease, from dyspepsia to dropsy! A Christianity without tears! In New England there was a hearty welcome for such a modernised form of the traditional religious beliefs without too close a scrutiny of its intellectual credentials.

It must not, however, be supposed that there was in the teaching of the Founder any suspicion of what is now technically known as modernism. Had Mrs. Eddy indulged in biblical criticism of the scientific type, had she challenged at any point the authority of the Scripture narrative, or attempted to apply the historical method to the interpretation of the sacred writings, she would have been given a very short shrift. She was far too prudent, or far too limited in her intellectual scope, to do any of these dangerous things. Her methods of handling the ancient literature belong to the age of Gregory the Great. The distinction which Matthew Arnold drew between literature and dogma does not exist for her. Every word of the Holy Writ is true, if not literally, then symbolically and mystically. When she finds a text convenient to her argument, she quotes it as scientific proof; when she is confronted with an apparent contradiction, she sails away upon the wings of a symbol, an analogy, a hidden or recondite significance.

In another matter also, she showed a prudent spirit of conservatism. Her teaching was marked by a deep vein of sincere Puritanism. Though she had liberated herself at an early age from the formidable terrors of the Calvinistic creed, she stood for temperance and strict living. Free love met with her stern disapproval. Celibacy was pronounced to be more blessed than marriage. By a concession to human frailty, the propagation of children in lawful wedlock was graciously permitted until "time matures human growth." In vague but impressive language the prophetess indicated that, if there were enough Christian Science in the world, there would be no more sin, or sickness, or death, and that the continuance of the human race would be assured without the dubious expedient of a fleshly union.

Yet even this attractive religious prospectus would not have sufficed to establish Christian Science against its many rivals had it not been for the unremitting vigilance and swift business instincts of the Founder. Having chosen her fighting ground, she dug deep trenches all around it. Mind-cures other than those of the approved variety were denounced as worse than useless. Animal magnetism was loaded with abuse. As for the established medical profession, it was sufficient to announce that "the reeling [*sic*] ranks of *materia medica,* with poisons, nostrums, and knives, are impotent to war with the omnipotent."

In the early days of the Church, when copies of the new Bible were comparatively scarce, the readers would not infrequently depend upon manuscript extracts from *Science and Health*. Mrs. Eddy was prompt to descry the dangers of this practice. If it were open to every reader to employ manuscript copies in the pulpit, how maintain the purchasing public for the book, or safeguard the doctrine from perversion or development? Quimby had been so lax as to allow his manuscripts to circulate among his pupils, and nobody was better able than Mrs. Eddy to appraise the consequences of this imprudence. That mistake at least should not be repeated. "It is not right," she wrote, "to copy my book and read it publicly without my consent." The teacher of a Christian Science class was enjoined to require every member to own a copy of *Science and Health,* and to continue the study of that text-book after the conclusion of the course.

It was wise to stake everything on the book. A day would come when the voice of the teacher would be silent, and the continuance of the Church would depend on the message of the printed word. So the lucrative Metaphysical College was closed, that its Founder, retiring from the arduous labours of the teacher, but also from "overwhelming prosperity," might devote her energies to the revision of the sacred work.

A series of spirited lawsuits had stemmed the volume of infringing publications (estimated to exceed three thousand), and had almost established for *Science and Health* a secured financial success. "The Ambassador of Christ's teaching upon earth," as she described herself, had no intention of appointing a successor or enduring a rival. Her controlling hand was on every spring of the machine. She intended to rule the Church, while she lived, through act and word, and for ever afterwards from her grave through the unimpeachable and unchallenged authority of *Science and Health*.

THE CREED

"Dollars and cents," observed Mr. Wiggins, her literary assistant, "she understands thoroughly"; but it was also part of her general business acumen that she could discern the drift of opinion and sail with the current. So, when the faithful Mrs. Corner was put on her trial for having procured the death of her daughter and grandchild by too literal an application of Christian, in lieu of obstetrical, Science, the Reverend Mother formally disclaimed responsibility. And thus, again, when the romantic Mrs. Woodbury, relying upon the doctrine that women might become mothers "by a supreme effort of their own mind" (and why not, matter being non-existent?), announced the immaculate birth of a son, to be known to the world as "The Prince of Peace," the Reverend Mother concluded that Mrs. Woodbury was no better than she should be, and promptly ejected her from the Church. Herein she displayed her wisdom. Repeated deaths in childbed would be bad; a regular flow of little Princes and Princesses of Peace would be worse for the rising reputation of a young institution. So the wayward and fanatical were crushed, and, by degrees, the rigour of the doctrine tempered to the unhappy times. The Christian Scientist was permitted to undergo vaccination (1901) and to consult medical practitioners in certain cases. Instruction in obstetrics was abandoned, and the healers were recommended to avoid the treatment of contagious or infectious ailments.

The High Priestess of Christian Science owes even less to literary style than the Founder of Positivism. Renan observed of Auguste Conte that he had been set up as a man of the highest order of genius for having said in bad French what all scientific thinkers for two hundred years had seen as clearly as himself. No scientific thinker in any age has ever seen what Mrs. Eddy saw. Christian Science is as eccentric as Positivism is commonplace; but Mrs. Eddy shares with Auguste Conte the distinction of belonging to that class of authors who have exercised a wide influence upon their generation, while owing nothing to the form in which they have cast their thoughts. Even by the standards of her own country, so much more indulgent to lax writing than France, Mrs. Eddy is gen-

THE CREED

erally adjudged to have had a very imperfect command of the English language. She has an unfortunate taste both in the selection and in the distribution of words. Through defects of education she is ignorant of the meaning of many of the more ambitious terms which it is her little vanity to employ. Her grammar is often seriously at fault. In the grace, the charm, the scholarly precision, which commend a writer to a wide circle of readers, she is completely deficient. Hers is the case of an author who has something serious to say, something which she believes to be of supreme importance to the whole human race, and to have been confided to her alone to communicate to the world, and yet so little tact has she in the management of the English language that she is capable of writing "hetacombs of gushing theories," and again, "Permit me to say that your Editorial in the August number is *par excellence*. It is a digest of good manners, morals, methods, means. It points to the scientific, spiritual molecule, pearl, and pinnacle, that everybody needs." In verse she is no less slovenly:

> 'Twas Love whose finger traced *aloud*
> A bow of primrose in the cloud!

Or again:

> Hope *happifies* life in the altar or bower,
> And loosens the fetters of pride and of power.

To travel through the five hundred pages of *Science and Health* is, indeed, to undertake an arduous pilgrimage. It is true that with the help of the Rev. Mr. Wiggins, of Harvard University, and other literary advisers, the English of the fifth and subsequent editions was chastened and improved, though not to the extent of eliminating those "hetacombs of gushing theories," which were afterwards explained by the authoress to be a piece of unappreciated humour. Yet if a certain external precision was thus imparted to the text, its essential substance and quality of style remained unaltered. Every page bears the unmistakable imprint of Mrs. Eddy's dogmatic but disjointed mental processes, of her passion for alliteration and verbal oppositions, of her straining after apocalyptic effects, and of her all-pervading logical weakness. Obscurity she cherished for its own sake. "She does not

THE CREED

care," wrote Mr. Wiggins, "to have her paragraphs clear, and delights in so expressing herself that her words may have various readings and meanings. That is one of the tricks of the trade." It was a trick as old as the Sibyl. Nevertheless, here and there among the blocks of dogmatic granite, which are strewn over the wastes of this extended homily, the traveller comes across a little oasis—a few sentences marked by eloquence and earnest feeling, a fine sentiment well expressed, a controversial thrust effectively delivered, a piece of shrewd common sense simply and plainly set out. Such, to the mere literary pilgrim, are the slender consolations of an itinerary conducted over difficult and baffling country in a rarefied atmosphere compounded of metaphysical paradox and religious mysticism, of practical hints to healers and far-fetched biblical exegesis.

It is not, however, to the arbiter of literary elegance that Mrs. Eddy addresses her message. In language which every citizen of the United States can understand she sets out the claim of her book to be regarded as a sovereign remedy for the ailments of mankind. "A thorough perusal of the author's publications heals sickness. If patients sometimes seem worse while reading this book, the change may either come from the alarm of the physician, or mark the crisis of the disease. Perseverance in its perusal has generally healed them completely." And, the better to advertise the medicinal properties of the volume, there is appended an imposing list of testimonials contributed by persons who have experienced the beneficial effects of *Science and Health*. One reader was impelled to give up tobacco and beer, and found, contrary to the prognostications of his wife, that the loss of his two old favourites added thirty pounds to his weight. A dyspeptic reports that after the perusal of the volume he can eat with impunity anything he wants. Dislocated hip, blood poisoning, curvature of the spine, lameness, profane language, the tobacco habit, the alcohol habit, neuralgia—*Science and Health* cures them all. Ten-pound Christian Science boys are produced "natural and safe," without suffering to the mother and babe, by the application of this valuable volume. It is little wonder that an anonymous correspondent in Chicago writes that "three dollars invested in *Science and Health* will be found the greatest financial investment of your life."

We have no doubt that these tributes to the curative properties of *Science and Health* are genuine. The patient who has paid three dollars for a talisman is predisposed to think that he has got value for his purchase. In many cases the talisman will work for no other reason than that it is expected to work. Anticipation ripens into faith, and faith supplies the precise psychological tonic which was needed to effect a cure. There must be many other cases in which Christian Science, like the moon, shines with a borrowed light. An improvement in the patient's condition is ascribed to the perusal of *Science and Health* on no stronger ground than sequence of time. *Post hoc, ergo propter hoc.* "After reading Mrs. Eddy I am cured, therefore Mrs. Eddy has cured me." A hundred other circumstances, each capable of exercising some influence on the patient's condition, are left out of account, either because they are not observed at all, or because, when brought into comparison with the lustre of a quasi-miracle, they appear to be humdrum and uninteresting. As is usual in the case of witnesses untrained in scientific observation, the negative instances are not reported. We have a florilegium of reputed successes, but no computation of admitted failures.

To attempt a detailed investigation of the cures attributed either to the perusal of Christian Science literature or to the ministrations of Christian Science healers would be a vast and profitless expenditure of labour. The evidence for these remedial triumphs has not been prepared for a court of law. Even when the witnesses may be acquitted of vulgar credulity, or of that tendency to deceive which is a note of the hysterical condition, they are not versed in the logic of evidence, so that while many cures may be authentic, the scrupulous historian will hesitate to pronounce that any one is proved.

There is the less reason to regret the lax and partisan way in which the evidence for these cures has been presented, because we are at once prepared to concede the authenticity of a certain proportion of the healings ascribed to

THE CREED

the operation of Christian Science. Which cures may be authentic, and which fictitious, we have no certain means of knowing, but that some cures are authentic is a legitimate inference from the acknowledged fact that the mind influences the body, and that other forms of mind-cure, more scientifically attested have undoubtedly yielded remarkable results. The imperfect manner, therefore, in which the evidence for these Christian Science healings is placed before the public must not lead us to suppose that healings never occur. Undoubtedly they do occur, though far less frequently than is alleged.

On the other side of the account there is a formidable balance of evil. With the effrontery which is the mark of imposture or fanaticism, Mrs. Eddy rejects the whole medical and surgical science of the world, not only as worthless, but as positively deleterious, and in this belief is followed by the precisians of her Church. It is impossible to compute the amount of unnecessary suffering, or the number of unnecessary deaths, which have been caused by this strange and suicidal perversity. Rather than invoke the aid of physical science, parents will freely sacrifice their children, and owners the dumb animals committed to their charge. There are probably few elderly persons among us who cannot recall the case of a precious life which has been ruthlessly immolated on the altar of Christian Science.

Why, then, it may be asked, does any sensible or intelligent being profess Christian Science? What is there in this extravagant form of idealism which attracts persons who are not, ordinarily speaking, regarded as cranks, and leads them to conclusions so repugnant to the general experience and wisdom of mankind? The answer is that amid much which is fantastic and false there is a central core which is true. While it is false that illness is unreal, it is true that some illnesses are caused, and others aggravated, by mental conditions which may be removed by spiritual cures. While it is false that no mental cure can be effective save when it is administered by a Christian Scientist, it is true that the serene confidence and composure of the Christian mystic may be a valuable element in the equipment of a spiritual healer. That courage and faith are powerful auxiliaries in the battle

THE CREED

for health, and that these qualities may be communicated to the patient by a wise friend in whose nature they are already implanted, are propositions which we are all prepared to accept. The value of a religion depends, not so much upon the intellectual quality of its doctrine, as upon the moral worth of those who profess it. Judged by this test, the new Church attains to an honourable level—higher perhaps than Protestantism in Bombay, higher no doubt than Romanism in Madras. From its arduous paradox of the unreality of sin, pain, sickness, and death, from its central belief in the all-pervading goodness of the Divine Mind, a number of devoted men and women have derived spiritual sustenance in their active and sometimes helpful ministrations. The spectacle of spiritual force is always impressive, and the Christian Science healers may commend their message by the sanctity of their lives and the integrity of their faith. Admiring what they are and do, and penetrated by the need of linking the inner life to a career of practical usefulness, there are some who forget to ask themselves the question whether a religion of courage is appropriately based upon a metaphysic of avoidance and fear.

Moreover, experience has shown that the precise metaphysical structure of a religion has very little to do with the width of its acceptance. The popularity of a religion is far more likely to be determined by the degree to which it responds to desire than by its closeness to the facts of life. The crudest absurdities have never deterred men and women from accepting a system which fills a want in their moral natures. What is desired is taken; what is uncomprehended is left aside.

There is even a certain value in doctrinal audacity. "Man," says Renan, "is born mediocre; he is only good for something when he dreams." The dream of Christian Science is that sickness and sin, pain and death, are themselves dreams, unreal emanations of an unreal mind and destined to disappear before the advancing sunlight of faith. What religion has made larger promises to mankind than this? What dreams have been more sanguine or defiant? And what edifice has ever been more vulnerable to the daily thrust of unpleasant fact?

THE CREED

In her interpretations of the Scriptures, Mrs. Eddy enjoys a preferential advantage of which she makes a full and liberal use. In the first verse of the twelfth chapter of Revelation it is written: "And there appeared a great wonder in heaven; a woman clothed with the sun, and the moon under her feet, and upon her head a crown of twelve stars." Who is this mysterious woman? Mrs. Eddy, meditating on the problem, was guided by an inner illumination to the view that the Being prefigured in the Apocalypse was, and could be, no other than the inspired authoress of *Science and Health*. An appendix establishes the flattering identification on grounds which appear to provoke no challenge from the faithful. Mrs. Eddy was "the great wonder in heaven, the woman clothed with the sun, and the moon under her feet, and upon her head a crown of twelve stars." Armed with such celestial credentials, an authoress may address herself with confidence to the interpretation of the Holy Writ.

The shape which Mrs. Eddy's confidence assumes may be illustrated by the following examples of her method. It would be difficult to find in the whole range of sacred literature a simpler thought, clothed in simpler words, than "Give us this day our daily bread"; but Mrs. Eddy is not content to take the prayer simply. Bread is material, unreal, a figment of mortal mind, a matter of indifference to Christian Scientists. No one should pray for bread, or, indeed, for any other material object. What, then, does the sentence mean? Mrs. Eddy has no doubts. It means, "Give us grace for the day; feed the familiar affections."

Her interpretations of the first two chapters of Genesis are even more surprising. "God caused a deep sleep to fall on Adam, and he slept." Now Adam, in Mrs. Eddy's system of symbolism, stands for error, just as Abel stands for watchfulness, and Abraham for fidelity; but Adam may also be regarded as a man, and accordingly the commentary on Gen. ii: 21 runs: "Here falsity, error, charges Truth, God, with inducing a sleep or hypnotic state in Adam in order to perform a surgical operation on him, and thereby to create woman; this is the first word of hypnotism." After this, it is not surprising to learn that the true deduction to be derived from the words in Isaiah, "the wolf also shall dwell with the lamb," is that "the animals created by God are not carnivorous."

It is not improbable that some part of the vogue of this unusual book may be due to the fact that it may be regarded in certain aspects as a feminist manifesto. "We have not so much authority in Divine science," observes the authoress, "for considering God masculine as for considering Him feminine." If "Jesus of Nazareth was the most scientific man that ever trod the globe," Mrs. Eddy was the most scientific woman. In language characterised by earnestness and vigour the case is put for a revision of the traditional view of the relations of the sexes. The rights of woman are placed upon an equality with those of men. The unfair discrimination between the sexes, which was then a mark of the legal system both in the United States and in Great Britain, is very justly attacked. "If a dissolute husband deserts his wife, certainly the wronged, and perchance impoverished, woman should be allowed to collect her own wages, enter into business agreements, hold real estate, deposit funds, and own her children free from interference." On this side of her apostolate, as also in her denunciation of alcohol, Mrs. Eddy was in advance of her times.

The promotion of feminine rights, though a strong, was, nevertheless, only a subordinate interest to the authoress of *Science and Health*. For one sentence which is devoted to these practical topics, or to the advocacy of a higher and more spiritual conception of marriage, there are a hundred dealing with theology or metaphysics. Here Mrs. Eddy is possessed of an idea which in every age has appealed to religious and speculative minds; it is that of the unity and omnipotence of the Divine Spirit. "Christianity," she writes, "is not a creed nor a system of ceremonies, nor a special gift from a ritualistic Jehovah; but a demonstration of Divine Love, casting out error and healing the sick."

Now to the American mind this simple, practical, unecclesiastical view of Christianity possessed great attractions. To be told that the true sacrament is not the symbolical act of the communion, but participation in the Divine life; to learn that salvation lies in the present, not in the future, and that heaven is not a place, but a Divine state of the soul; to be advised that those are in error who think that spirit is born of matter and returns to matter, or that man experiences a resurrection from the dust, seeing that he is the spiritual and eternal reflection of God, and that it is only "man's counterfeit" that suffers, sins, and dies—above all, to realise that the sovereign truth, which avails to heal man of his imagined ailments, can be acquired by any devout and unlettered woman after a few hours of instruction—these ideas appealed to many who were beginning to find the traditional forms and doctrines of the Church meaningless, or obstructive to freedom, or out of tune with the thought of the modern world.

Moreover, despite many repellent ebullitions of arrogance and vulgarity, there is in several parts of the book a genuine devotional atmosphere, which has secured for its author a real measure of respect. When Mrs. Eddy, in one of those viciously florid ebullitions which are characteristic of her way of writing, says of the flowers of the field, "the floral apostles are the hieroglyphs of Deity," we are simply disgusted. It is difficult to believe that a woman who can endure to print such pretentious rubbish can be sincere in any part of her being. Yet Mrs. Eddy, despite her many unpleasant moral and intellectual qualities, was unquestionably a devout woman. Religion was the great concern of her life, and occasionally she can write of religion simply and in a way which stirs the sympathy of her reader. Here, for instance, is a chapter on prayer which bears the mark of a devout and sincere nature:

> In order to pray aright we must enter the closet and shut the door. We must close the lips, and silence the material senses. In the quiet sanctuary of earnest longings we must deny sin and plead God's allness. We must resolve to take up the cross, and go forth with honest hearts to work and watch for wisdom, truth, and love. We must pray without ceasing. Such prayer is answered, inasmuch as we put our desires into practice. The Master's injunction is that we pray in secret, and let our words attest our sincerity.

There is a certain class of mind, not very profound or intellectual or well balanced, which is attracted to a new form of religion by the violence and novelty of its challenge to admitted evils or familiar ways. The ugly and

THE CREED 129

depressing side of materialism was specially prominent in the society in which Mrs. Eddy passed her active life. To many simple folk, to whom the consolations of literature and art were foreign, the emptiness of the ordinary low-minded life had become an oppression. In their soulless desolation they found comfort in Christian Science. It asked them to believe that two persons, one a man born more than eighteen hundred years ago in Nazareth, Galilee, Asia, the other a woman born very recently at Bow, N.H., U.S.A., had been jointly entrusted with a revelation of supreme spiritual importance for the human race. They learned not only that matter was bad, but that it was unreal; not only that man was capable of improvement, but that, being made in the image of God, he was Divine and immortal. They learned that the life of the spirit was all in all; that the things which human beings were accustomed to regard as most real were, in truth, phantoms of a perishable intelligence, while that which they were wont to consider to be most distant and impalpable was, in fact, the only real and the only solid. It was not required of the believers that they should be clever, or learned, or accomplished. It was sufficient that they should have and live the faith. Miracles would not be lacking to corroborate the Church. The sick would be healed and the dying restored to health.

A new cure soon becomes fashionable. The application of "truth," as defined by Christian Science, to the treatment of disease was certainly a novelty. "Sickness," observes Mrs. Eddy, "has been fought for centuries by doctors using material remedies; but the question arises, 'Is there less sickness because of these practitioners?' A vigorous 'No' is the response deducible for two connate [*sic*] facts —the reputed longevity of the antediluvians, and the rapid multiplication and increased violence of diseases since the flood."

Such is the logic and such the history which the Founder invokes in support of her creed.

III

THE CHURCH

> Dy-na-mo, Dy-na-mo!
> We're the bunch, we're the bunch,
> Dy-na-mo!
> We're alive and coming,
> And we'll keep them humming.
> We're surely always on the go.

Les religions valent par les peuples qui les acceptent.
—RENAN.

THE CHURCH

IT was in August 1879 that, profiting by the indulgent laws of Massachusetts, Mrs. Eddy obtained a charter for her Church. She was then fifty-eight years of age, the authoress of a very long, tedious, and apparently quite unsaleable work, which had been several times refused by the publishers to whom it had been offered, and was only finally accepted because two zealous pupils were willing to make a substantial contribution to the cost of publication. She was a woman with no distinguished or wealthy connections, not rich enough to command domestic help, and the wife of a husband who had, in the previous year, been subjected to the humiliating torture of a malicious prosecution for murder.

By this time, it is true, she had gathered around her a band of disciples, but they were few in number and lowly in station. She would hold little services in Boston to congregations of twenty-five, thirty, fifty, preaching for a fee, and sending her docile little husband round with the collection plate. Yet she was not daunted. Though the original charter members were but twenty-six in number, and there was no money for a Church building, she carried through the business of getting a charter for the first Church of Christ Scientist.

Sixteen years pass. The unsaleable book is in its seventy-first edition, and its authoress is one of the most prosperous writers of her age. It has, moreover, been discovered, as far back as 1888, that this book, which the publishers rejected, is not merely a "best-seller," but that it occupies a unique place among the "best-sellers" of the world. *Science and Health*—such was now the authorised announcement—had been immaculately conceived. Mary Baker had equalled, perhaps even eclipsed, that other Mary of whose prominence in the regard and devotion of womankind she had been dimly and uncomfortably aware. There

THE CHURCH

could be no rivalry between the two Marys now. By her union with God, Mary Baker had brought forth, not a man-child, but what was much more appropriate to an intellectual age —a substantial book selling first at two dollars fifty cents, then at three dollars, later at three dollars eighteen cents, and, at each of these handsome prices devoured by an eager public. Meanwhile money had been pouring into the Christian Science till from many quarters— from the sales of *Science and Health,* from teaching, from the commissions paid by healers, from newspapers, from the annual minimum tribute of a dollar imposed upon all the faithful. A great church—the Mother Church, as it was called—is opened at Boston, a fabric of imposing size and costliness, stoutly built and softly cushioned—a seven million dollar church, according to a somewhat later computation, taking account of the value of its land and endowments; the kind of church which only the prosperous think of building, and only the prosperous are greatly attracted to attend.

In one gift only was the Mother Church lacking. By a series of crafty machinations it had been wholly deprived of liberty. The land upon which the church stood had been acquired by Mrs. Eddy; the fabric was the property of Mrs. Eddy; the governing corporation was named by Mrs. Eddy. The Mother Church was not a free body, but a close corporation legally bound to see that nothing was taught within its orbit save what might be found in the seventy-first and subsequent editions of *Science and Health,* upon pain of forfeiting the fabric and the land to Mrs. Eddy and her heirs.

In his amusing book on Christian Science, Mark Twain drew attention to the fact that the government of the new church was an unlimited autocracy. The Pastor Emeritus, as Mrs. Eddy is described in the *Church Manual,* appoints the five members of the Board of Directors, the President, the Treasurer, and the Clerk of the Board, the officials of the Publishing Society, the manager of the Committee on Publication, the editor and the managers of the Christian Science papers, the members of the Finance Committee, the members of the Business Committee. All these officials hold office at her pleasure. She may dismiss them without a word of explanation, as she may veto a publication or excommunicate a member for malpractice.

The autocracy was widely and relentlessly executed. Preaching was forbidden; writing was dangerous. Even to publish a defence of Christian Science was to invite a charge of heresy and to incur a risk of expulsion. Literature was the enemy. The theory was that the Christian Scientist had all the literature which was beneficial in the Bible and the writings of Mrs. Eddy.

To give personal service to the leader was an honour which no Christian Scientist might decline. At two days' notice any member of three years' standing or upwards might be ordered, on pain of excommunication, to serve in Mrs. Eddy's household for a period of more than three years. "He that loveth father and mother more than me is not worthy of me" was the text quoted in support of this astonishing manifestation of authority.

The death of the Pastor Emeritus made no change in the creed, constitution, or ritual of the Christian Science Church. Like the death of Napoleon at St. Helena, it was not an event, but merely news. Long before the venerable lady fell into that fatal "error" of pneumonia which removed her from the world she had made all the necessary dispositions for the perpetuation of the system which was the creature of her remarkable powers. The sacred book, after many revisions, had received its ultimate shape; the governing ordinances of the Church, under the modest designation of by-laws, had been gathered into a manual which was not to be altered save with the author's consent, and these by-laws the Mother Church in Boston was bound under its trust deed to observe. Though the government of the Church was thoroughly autocratic, it was so constituted that the disappearance of the supreme figure could make no sensible difference to its working. The powers nominally vested in the Reverend Mother had long, in effect, been exercised by a Board of Directors. Five well-dressed, level-headed, substantial North Americans, such as would grace any club window in Beacon Street, continued to carry on the old firm in the old way and under the old prospectus.

THE CHURCH

No heroic memories are associated with the names of Archibald McLellan, Allison V. Stewart, John V. Dittimore, Adam H. Dickey, and James A. Neal, the five directors appointed in 1904, upon whose shoulders was now imposed the sole responsibility for the direction of the growing Church. Their function was not to preach a faith, still less to endure a martyrdom, but to preserve and extend an institution by a strict attention to discipline and finance. The Pastor Emeritus had seen to it that their position should be unassailable and their powers as extensive as her own. The five directors hold their offices for life, and name their successors. Nobody can be admitted a member of the Mother Church, nobody registered as a healer, without their approval. They appoint to the Church offices and administer the Church funds. Since no branch Church can be organised without the consent of the Mother Church, and since the Mother Church is ruled by the Board of Five, these five business men, sitting in a well-appointed office in Boston, control the development of Christian Science activities all over the world. They can authorise a new Church;

they can dissolve an old one, they can excommunicate a heretic. Every address delivered by the travelling lecturers of the Church has passed the Boston censorship.

The longer the Church is studied, the more conscious do we become of the continuing influence of its remarkable Founder. There is Mrs. Eddy's mind in the Christian Science Movement, and there is no subsequent mind. Even now, despite the prodigious development of physical science, and the growth, more particularly since the war, of the science and art of mental healing, the doctrines and practice of this religion remain as Mrs. Eddy shaped them, and meant them to be. The Founder is dead, but directs the Church from her grave. The idea of development, the conception of theology as a progressive body of thought about ultimate realities taking up into itself the religious experience of mankind, was foreign to the mind of the Reverend Mother. For her, absolute truth was graven for all time on the immortal pages of *Science and Health,* those pages from the first so fully inspired, yet, strange to relate, so frequently

THE CHURCH

revised. It was for the faithful to accept, not to challenge or innovate. So under the modern directorate all new thought is firmly discouraged. It is because thought is dangerous that preaching is discountenanced, because controversy is dangerous that public debating is prohibited, because change is dangerous that the latest editions of the *Church Manual* continue to assume that the Pastor Emeritus is still active, and must not be molested in her drives abroad. An engaging flow of homiletic literature, issuing for the most part from the busy pens of enthusiastic American ladies, fills the pages of the authorised periodicals of the Church. It is not in this monthly pæan of praise that we should look for a note of criticism, dissent, or innovation.[1]

So this powerful and wealthy corporation, with its great newspaper interests, its monopoly of Christian Science literature, its annual tribute from the faithful, can afford to taste the comforts of tranquillity, and is as

---

[1] The repeated revision of a book immaculately conceived is a theological problem which attracts the notice of the *Christian Science Journal* for March 1891, "Did Paul or John," it is asked, "ever think of getting out a revised edition of their works"?

little susceptible to the *odium theologicum* as the Standard Oil Trust or the Bank of England. It is true that a well-directed publicity department is alert to discuss and reply to any strictures upon the Church or its Founder which may appear in the Press, and that the Board itself is not wholly silent. From time to time the directors will publish a communiqué in answer to criticisms, or a vindication of the orthodox Christian Science position; but the tone of these defensive documents is prudent and restrained. Occasions of cerebral excitement are carefully avoided; the zeal of the proselyte is warned off Roman Catholic ground; public devotions are restricted to four regular occasions in the week. Stress is laid upon the quiet work of the healer rather than upon ceremonies, processions, and controversial displays.

No small part of the singular stability enjoyed by the Church must be attributed to its sound financial position. Had Christian Science remained the religion of the poor shoemakers of Lynn, it would doubtless have split into a thousand sects, each thinking apart, and differing in some minute point of practice or worship from the other; but at Mrs. Eddy's death the Church was already wealthy, and a legacy from the Founder of two million five hundred thousand dollars greatly added to its financial strength. It is natural that the Board of Directors at Boston, who control the machine and regulate its working, should seek to avoid innovations, which cannot but impair the good-will of a flourishing concern. The prosperous do not seek out quarrels, or run after intellectual adventures. They enjoy what they have, and ask only for a period of tranquillity in which to increase it.

In nothing does the worldly prudence of the Christian Science directorate more clearly exhibit itself than in its conduct of the newspapers which sustain and diffuse the influence of the faith. Let it be said at once in their praise that they are honest and clean of offence, and that the *Christian Science Monitor,* a great daily, is, on the side of information, most admirably equipped. But, just as the discerning reader can pick out a coloured newspaper by the prevalence of its undertakers, advertisements, or by its profuse reference to

Baptist services, or, again, by the prominence which it assigns to news from Liberia, so the *Christian Science Monitor,* despite the excellence of its foreign news, betrays its origin and limitations. The editors—"immaculately dressed," as we are assured by one who knows them—decline to acknowledge the existence of evil, rule out death, and illness, and crime, and the furies of party warfare. The *Monitor* has none of these things—no obituary columns, no sensations of the police court, no party politics, not a paragraph calculated to arouse painful, melancholy, or vindicative thoughts. A whole side of human experience is deliberately blotted out from the purview of this efficient and admirable newspaper. Yet the financial consequences of this serious omission are not unfavourable. The editors are well advised in thinking that there is a large public, not only in the United States but throughout the world, who do not wish to have their feelings unnecessarily harrowed, and are the readier to pay for a daily dose of information if it can be served up to them with every species of cheerful condiment which the editorial art can supply.

THE CHURCH

The existence of a daily newspaper of this type, which is read and valued on its merits by thousands of intelligent people who are not interested in Christian Science, as such, helps the Church. The propaganda is there—for no number appears without a quotation from Mrs. Eddy's writings—but it is not obtruded in such a way as to offend the profane who resort to the *Monitor* for their daily information. The result is that many who would not ordinarily be interested in Christian Science, and have no intention of reading the distinctive literature of the Church, are brought within the range of Christian Science influence. If they are proof against the doctrine, they are yet disposed to think indulgently of a Church which can put a good daily journal on the breakfast table. "Can it be," they ask, "that an enterprise so sober and lucrative has sprung from the root of crazed and illiterate superstition?"

Yet in the course of every calendar year there is one day at least in which the *Monitor* appears in its full Christian Science uniform. The annual meeting of the Mother Church in

Boston is largely attended, and the report of its proceedings covers several pages of the *Monitor*. The Presidential address, the report of the Treasurer, of the Auditor, of the Trustees under the will of Mary Baker Eddy, of the Board of Lectureship, of the Committee on Publication, of the Publishing Society, of the Benevolent Association, of the Clerk, of the Sunday School, are printed, if not in their entirety, at least with great fullness, so that the devout all the world over may have an opportunity of appreciating how the Church stands, and what progress it has made during the past year.

Let it not for a moment be imagined that in such a gathering of Christian Scientists there is any note of tumult or ecstasy, such as often disfigured the early councils of the Christian Church, or marks the revivalist movements of our own age. The Christian Science community has long passed out of its temperamental stage and is now comfortable, quiet, orderly. The appeal of its preceptors is pragmatic and utilitarian. The religion is good for health, good for business, sweetens social relations. "It is known," observes the

THE CHURCH

Hon. William W. Davis (June 2nd, 1929), "to many business and professional men that the increasing demand for higher ethical standards in business is due in great measure to the impetus given by those who are students of Christian Science. Through their example better methods are being used, sharp practices are being abandoned, and misrepresentations and extortions no longer lead to success." The great annual stocktaking of the Church, which reminds us of the annual meeting of a commercial company, encourages the shareholders to persevere in a flourishing and growing concern. If no formal vote of confidence in the directorate is passed, the sentiment of confidence is none the less expressed. "We gratefully accept," observes the President, "every opportunity to renew our loyalty to the Board of Directors who steadfastly uphold the *Manual* and the teachings of Christian Science."

The liturgy of the Church bears the trace, not of growth, but of manufacture. The Reverend Mother has seen to every detail. She has written a spiritual interpretation of the Lord's

Prayer. She has settled the length of the voluntary and the post-lude; she has prescribed —what is the most audacious feature of the ceremony—the reading at every Sunday service or Wednesday meeting of the selected passages from *Science and Health*. After a lesson from the Bible has been read by the Second Reader, the First Reader says the following words: "As announced in the explanatory note, I shall now read correlative passages from the Christian Science text-book, *Science and Health, with Key to the Scriptures,* by Mary Baker Eddy." The source of the second lesson must not for a moment be left in ambiguity. With provident insistence Mrs. Eddy has secured that the title of her book and the name of its author should be specially mentioned on each occasion.

In this ritual there is little calculated to appeal to the æsthetic temperament. There are no candles, no vestments, no chants, no crucifixes or images, no incense, no delicate movements of priests or acolytes, no tinkling of bells, no sacramental mysteries—nothing of the poetry, the sentiment, the hieratic pomp of an ancient religion. The opportunities for

THE CHURCH 149

prayer are rigorously curtailed. Sermons are forbidden. Of an apostolic succession not a vestige. There is no ornamental hierarchy, no material symbols such as bread and wine. The Readers, male and female, are chosen for a period of years, and discharge their function of reading lessons from the Bible and Mrs. Eddy, not as priests endowed with sacred credentials from on high, but as ordinary members of the congregation, habited in their mundane clothes. There is an organ. In its businesslike way the *Church Manual* lays down that the music of the Mother Church "shall not be operatic, but of an appropriate religious character and of a recognised standard of musical excellence." There are also hymns, and the welcome aid of a soloist. To a limited degree the music is invoked to relieve the plain prose of a service which is a good deal nearer to the Congregationalist than to the Roman model.

Yet this prevailingly jejune worship is not without its popular and even sensational tonics. At the Wednesday meeting the congregation are invited to proclaim their experiences and testimonies, and to offer remarks on Christian Science. At these weekly services the courage of the faithful is refreshed by a flowing stream of arresting narratives in illustration of the healing power of the new philosophy. The tedium of an established liturgy is broken by fresh jets of spontaneous enthusiasm. Miraculous cures are recounted, with their very human details, and many an intimate page of our common nature is exhibited as on a screen to an interested audience.

There can be little question that the incorporation of this element of public testimony into the formal services of the Christian Science Church constitutes a distinct and important attraction. No one can tell in advance who may rise and testify, or what particular form the testimony may take. The doctrine which comes from above is never so alluring as the evidence which comes from below. To a Christian Science audience an ounce of miracle is worth a ton of argument. The testimonies supply an assurance that the work in the mission field progresses, and that the healers are bringing home their sheaves.

To the impartial critic the evidence which is brought forward on these occasions will

THE CHURCH 151

seem to be of little value. The patient who attests that she has been cured by a Christian Science healer is no independent witness. She does not only assign merit to the healer; a good share of the imputed glory belongs to herself. To be cured of sickness, seeing that sickness is error, is itself a sign of grace and a mark of enlightenment. The person who is sufficiently well disposed to Christian Science to have trust in a healer will be more than half impelled, out of self-respect, to announce a cure. If it is right to be Christian, and if it is Christian to be healed, then it is right to be healed. It is a sound rule always to discount evidence which redounds to the credit of the witness.

It is not, however, of impartial critics that this Church is composed, but, in the main, of good, enthusiastic women. If the supreme business management is in competent male hands, the work of teaching and healing is chiefly carried on by females. For one male practitioner in England there are seven of the opposite sex. In Boston, males and females are more balanced—four women to one man. In Chicago there are ninety-one males to five hundred and fifty women—a proportion of one man to six women.

The fact that it was set up by a woman helps to explain the special appeal of the Christian Science Church in those Protestant communities where the feminist spirit is strongly developed, or where there is a marked statistical preponderance of the female sex. "Consider for a moment," writes a woman lecturer authorised by the Board of Lectureship of the Mother Church, "the wonder of this woman's life. From birth she had been delicate, and at the age of fifty-five she was a frail invalid, overcome by the least exertion. At that age she made her great discovery, and it changed her from an invalid to a woman of marvellous energy and endurance. When over fifty she brought out her first great work, *Science and Health, with Key to the Scriptures*. At the same time she was healing cases of so-called chronic and incurable disease of every description. She was healing diseases, and organising her students into bands to go out into all the world and heal the sick. Finally she undertook the greatest and most arduous task of all—the founding of the Christian Church,

THE CHURCH 153

the Mother Church with all its activities. No woman had ever founded a Church before, far less had any woman been the inspired leader of a scientific and religious movement. In achieving this she lifted all womankind for ever."

In this pæan of praise there is one sentence which is incontestably true. "No woman had ever founded a Church before." In this field Mrs. Eddy had broken every record, and the semi-divine honours which, in a bustling and excitable community, are so freely accorded to the man who first reached the North Pole or flew the Atlantic are naturally lavished upon the woman who first founded a Church. Moreover, in reviving the idea of healing through religion, Mrs. Eddy opened out to the members of her own sex a wide field of congenial ministration and activity. The woman healer in the Church of Christ Scientist is the pendant to the father confessor in the Roman Communion. She receives the spiritual (and physical) confidences of her patients and administers in her turn the soothing consolations of her faith. Many a solitary, half-employed woman welcomes into her empty life such an ally—not exactly a doctor, not exactly a parson, but a blithe professional optimist of her own sex, who can draw at any moment from a bank of idealistic philosophy a shower of glittering and sanguine reflections as to the allness of God, the perfection of man, and the nothingness of matter, and lift her straight out of the pit of despondency on to a higher level of courage and hope. The attraction of a spiritual relationship of this kind appears in many cases to be great. Yet the relationship is seldom purely spiritual. It is usual for cash to pass. The Reverend Mother, who was nothing if not practical, strongly encouraged the notion that cash should pass. The healers were enjoined to make charges equal to those of reputable physicians in their localities. On no other terms would they secure the respect of a competitive society unaccustomed to the idea that something can be gained for nothing. In this calculation Mrs. Eddy displayed her habitual prudence. "The perfect thoughts of a perfect mind" must be given a cash value. Otherwise no good American citizen would believe that they would cure so much as a toothache. So it

THE CHURCH 155

is not merely a fresh mission field, but a new and not ungainful profession, that the Reverend Mother has opened out to the women of the world. The earnings of the practitioner may not be great—though we are assured that an income of 5,000 dollars a year and upwards is now enjoyed by at least twenty-five practitioners in Boston—but they are not to be despised, and are sufficient to attract labourers to the vineyard.

What the exact number of these practitioners may be, and how many patients annually seek their aid, are matters with regard to which we have no precise knowledge. An American writer stated in 1912 that there were then ten thousand Christian Science healers in the United States, and an annual supply of some six million Christian Science patients. If these were true figures for 1912, the figures now must be considerably higher. What is certain is that a large number of people, not members of the Church, occasionally visit a Christian Science healer as an experiment or for some special form of nervous disorder, and that so the Church spreads its filaments far beyond the circle of its registered membership.

To enter a Christian Science church in London is at once to exchange the old England for the new. There is no cheaper voyage across the Atlantic than to step off the pavement into one of these dignified, well-appointed, hospitable buildings, wit hits atmosphere of solid comfort and thoroughly capable management, its freedom from any sense of awe and solemnity, its close adjustment to the practical needs of a practical community. Is it a church? Is it a social meeting-place? Is it a Sunday school? Is it a publisher's emporium? Is it a curative agency? Is it a school for proselytes? It is all of these things, and no one of them exclusively. At a counter in the entrance-hall we may find a well-dressed lady dispensing the literature of the Christian Science publishing society at the current prices. In the reading-room—and the reading-room is no accidental feature of a Christian Science Church, but an institution definitely ordained to fulfill an important purpose—the reader finds displayed the writings of Mrs. Eddy in morocco bindings, the concordance of *Science and Health* (611 pages), the concordance of Mrs. Eddy's writings other than *Science and Health* (1,103 pages), the *Church Manual,* the *Christian Science Monitor,* the *Christian Science Journal* (with its motto, "Heal the Sick, Raise the Dead, Cleanse the Lepers, Cast out Demons"), the *Sentinel,* the *Quarterly, Der Herold,* (German-English), and *Le Héraut* (French and English). Here is abundant pasture for the neophyte: the little poems and sermons by American ladies in the *Journal;* the names and addresses of practitioners who may be consulted; testimonies of healing, reported by the brisk and most businesslike Boston publishing house, to be duly verified; and, for the stronger digestions, the vast ramifications of Mrs. Eddy herself. The Christian Science publishing firm does its work well. In the art of pushing its sales and securing advertisements from nurses and practitioners it need fear no rivalry.

Let us venture into one of these London churches soon after noon on Wednesday. The street, quiet enough in general at this hour of the day, suddenly wakes up to life. Motorcars and taxis discharge smartly dressed ladies before the steps which lead up to the august portals of the First, Second, Third, etc., Church of Christ Scientist, as the case may be, and these are mingled with converging streams of eager-looking pedestrians, mostly of the female sex. For a few minutes the members of the congregation chat with one another pleasantly in the spacious entrance-hall, and then by degrees drift into the church, a large lozenge-shaped room admirably constituted for sound, with, at one end, a graded hemicycle of seats, and at the other, in place of an altar, an organ, and before it a platform bearing two handsomely carved lecterns, one for the Bible, the other for Mrs. Eddy's *Science and Health.* Everything in this spacious and well-furnished room indicates wealth. Not that there are images, pictures, or crucifixes, or, save for two texts, any mural decorations; but a moment's inspection of the solid and finished workmanship of the building is sufficient to show that the absence of ornament is not the consequence of any lack of material means, but a reminder that Christian Science sprang from a Puritan root, and still contains, amid all its ample provisions, something of that simple, old-world atmosphere which we breathe in the pages of the Blythesdale romance.

When the last strains of the voluntary have died away, the church is reasonably full. There are a few men, and a sprinkling of children brought by their mothers, but the great bulk of those present consist of women of the upper and middle classes, and of these the majority appear to be in the middle stage of life, and neurasthenic.

The service begins. A grey-haired lady, solid, composed, and dignified, steps on to the platform from behind, advances to the desk on the left hand, and reads out the words of the first hymn. It happens to be Mrs. Eddy's:

> Shepherd, show me how to go
> Over the hillside steep,
> How to gather, how to sow,
> How to feed Thy sheep.
> I will listen for thy Voice,
> Lest my footsteps stray;
> I will follow and rejoice
> All the rugged way.

After the hymn has been read from end to end, the whole congregation—for there is no choir, surpliced or unsurpliced—sing it with real feeling. There follow in succession the lesson from the Bible, and the lesson from *Science and Health,* read with equal reverence by the lady Reader. The lesson from *Science and Health,* which is the *pièce de résistance* of the service, enumerates the different types of ailment which Christian Science is competent to cure. These readings duly accomplished, there is a short period for silent prayer, the congregation remaining seated, followed by the Lord's Prayer, read aloud by the Reader, and repeated by the congregation. Then follows another hymn.

From this point the service enters a stage of very great human interest. The Reader announces that the time has come for testimonies and remarks. It is a very general experience at public meetings that when the audience is asked to make a contribution, either by way of question or observation, an awkward interval of silence intervenes. No such awkward interval is interposed here. The witnesses are straining like greyhounds on the leash. There are funds of latent eloquence in the bosoms of these grateful and enthusiastic votaries. One after another they rise from doubtedly an error to conjure up this depressing memory of an injured parent, for when, by a mental effort, that memory had been expelled, the swelling by degrees abated. Another lady observed that she had always been greatly impressed by Mrs. Eddy's observation that accidents are unknown to God. Not long ago she had spilt some methylated spirit. There was an alarming blaze of fire, and at first it looked very much as if an accident had occurred; but then she recollected how the dear leader had said that there were no accidents, and from the moment that true thought came into her mind the fire died away, and she was able, by stamping upon it, to extirpate what remained. It did not apparently occur to this witness that the methylated spirit might have been consumed.

An eager young metaphysician then rose to throw light upon one of the most delicate problems of Christian Science practice—the relief of dumb animals. This young lady had a friend, and the young lady's friend had a dog, and the dog of the young lady's friend was sick, and its owner—horrid thought!—contemplated invoking the aid of a veterinary

THE CHURCH

different parts of the hall, and for the most part discharge themselves with great ease and volubility. It is clear that a confession *coram publico* has powerful allurements, for be it observed that it is a confession, not of sins, but of virtues, not of failures, but of successes, and that to bear witness in a congregation of the faithful is an act, not of penitence, but of pride. A well-dressed young lady rose at once to express her gratitude to the Church for these Wednesday morning meetings, so convenient to country members, and also for the very remarkable manner in which, during a recent gale in the Bay of Biscay, she had been, through science, preserved from seasickness. Then followed a handsome confession of error. An elderly lady had been hit in the cheek by falling timber. There was pain. There was swelling. How were these things possible? The elderly lady remembered that she was in error. The blow upon her cheek had, owing to the law of association of ideas, reminded her of a similar but more serious accident which had befallen her father. He too had been struck by falling timber, and had in consequence lost the sight of one eye. It was un-

THE CHURCH

surgeon. "Give me," cried the pious young lady, "till midday, and if the dog be not cured by midday, call for this surgeon if you must." Now the young lady, being a scientist, was very metaphysical. She began to think what a dog really was, how a dog would have appealed to Mrs. Eddy. A dog was not a hairy thing on four legs. It was a bundle of spiritual qualities—gratitude, fidelity, obedience, and the like. The important thing in the healing of a dog is not to attend to its unreal material aspect but to concentrate the mind on its spiritual qualities, and this the young lady did, with such remunerative effect that by midday the dog, though still limping a little, was capable of barking with renewed animation.

Hardly had the congregation recovered from the effects of this miracle, than it was invited to contemplate the spectacle of a Russian Prince beggared by the recent revolution, of a Prince so impoverished that he was compelled to seek a livelihood by the practice of the carver's art. Now this Prince had the good fortune to meet in Germany the narrator, an American lady, firmly rooted in the faith; and though the Prince knew no English, and the American lady was unable to speak Russian, by the friendly good offices of an interpreter the two were enabled to converse with one another, the Russian Prince enlarging on his pecuniary needs, the American lady on the advantages of Christian Science, and each so much interested in the other that they did not separate till three o'clock in the morning. The consequence of this interchange was remarkably gratifying to each of its participants. The Prince very shortly afterwards received a substantial cheque from one who owed him money, and the lady did not fail to remind him of the Divine source of this unexpected aid. Whether the Prince was suitably impressed, whether from that moment he resolved to desert the Orthodox faith and to apply for admission to the Church of Christ Scientist, we were not told. The moral, however, was clear, Christian Science collects the debts of impoverished and deserving Russian princes who have the good fortune to meet travelling American ladies of the true faith.

A tall young man, recently cured of neurasthenia, and now engaged in some department of salesmanship, then rose to explain to the

THE CHURCH 165

congregation how one day when trade was slack, and he had come to the conclusion that "nothing was doing," and was, in fact, about to take train for the suburbs—at the eleventh hour, as it were, he obtained unexpectedly, and through the fostering help of Christian Science, a welcome contract. Not only, then, does this religion arrest seasickness, cure dogs, suppress accidents from fire, and collect debts; it actively brings business to the salesman.

The time allotted to these confessions (which were listened to by the congregation with grave attention) was now at an end. The Reader announced a third hymn, and, when this had been sung, gave out the necessary business notices relating to services, lectures, new reading-rooms, and the like. Then the audience dispersed, some stopping to buy the authorised Christian Science literature at the bookstall, others to chat and compare notes in the hall and portico before they streamed out into the roar and bustle of London, to banish the false belief of an appetite by the unreal and unnecessary phantom of a lunch.

There is one thing which sharply distinguishes the history of Christian Science from that of many other religions which have enlisted the interest or conquered the souls of men. Christian Science has never endured persecution. Nowhere in the world is there, or has there been a Christian Science martyr. The frowns of the medical profession and the rivalries of competing mind-cures have been the worst obstacles to the smooth advance of this new religion. In the easy, tolerant atmosphere of the United States the revelation of Mrs. Eddy has been received with a composure bred of a long and varied experience of religious crazes. And why not? The Christian Scientist does not, like the Mormon, offend public morals. He is a good American citizen, believing in George Washington, the Constitution, and Abraham Lincoln. No one can plead that his doctrine is subversive of property or likely to depress the price of rails or rubber. If in certain points the Christian Science practitioner runs counter to some provision of the law, the State legislatures of the Union are susceptible to pressure from those who know how pressure should be brought to

THE CHURCH 167

bear. Now it is the function of the committees on Christian Science publications to watch the legislatures of the world and to see that they take no action adverse to the interests of their creed. A remarkable shower of legislative blessings rewards this diligent vigilance. In more than forty states of the Union provision is now made for Christian Science, either explicitly or in general terms. Some states tolerate, others actually confer privileges upon, the new religion. In Oregon the Christian Science practitioner is exempted from jury service, in Arkansas from the ordinary medical examinations. Nor are these concessions confined to the United States. Even in England, Christian Science nursing-homes have since 1927 been exempted from the ordinary regulation which required the supervision of a qualified medical practitioner or medically trained nurse.

This swift measure of success would hardly, one would think, have been possible had there been anything in the new religion calculated seriously to alarm or offend. Such, however, has not been the case. Even if the strength of Christian Science may not lie in good taste or good sense, the women who form the rank and file of the Christian Science army cannot be said to constitute a public peril, or an affront to the decencies of life. Indeed, it is probable that the level of private conduct among Christian Scientists is as high as that which prevails among other bodies of practising Church people in the United States, and higher than that of the average voter. Nor is the movement altogether unconnected with the advancement of great and honourable causes. It is to the honour of the Founder that, despite the opposition of her relations, she was a stout and insistent opponent of Southern slavery. To-day the *Christian Science Monitor* has come forward as the champion of peace and disarmament; and it is noticeable that in recent years the Church has countered the charge of indifference to distress which was sometimes brought against it by organising relief works in the scenes of great calamities, as when Corinth was wrecked by an earthquake, Florida devastated by a hurricane, or Alabama overwhelmed by the flooding waters of the Mississippi.

We may, notwithstanding, conjecture that

THE CHURCH

without Mrs. Eddy's prudent guidance the new religion might easily have encountered a formidable, perhaps an insuperable, show of opposition. If the Christian Science healers had been encouraged to force their ministrations upon unwilling or unknowing patients, if an idea had been spread abroad that there was within the community a body of persons claiming semi-divine powers, who, whether you liked it or no, were working for your welfare or your ill, the patience even of the good-natured American public might have given way. The Pastor Emeritus had foreseen this danger, this peril of "obtrusive mental healing," and provided against it. "I insist," she wrote, "on the etiquette of Christian Science as well as its morals [sic] and religion," and in an article in the *Journal* she pronounced it to be a breach both of good morals and good manners to treat patients without their knowledge or consent. By imposing this curb upon the aspiring spirit of her zealous followers Mrs. Eddy undoubtedly conferred a benefit on the Church.

The spread of Christian Science in the United States has been so rapid as, in some quarters, to engender the fear that the political direction of the republic, might ultimately, fall into the hands of the members of this well-meaning but fantastic sect. Christian scientists may rule a state; not so Christian Science. No community of men and women governed on strict Christian Science principles could hold together for a year. An American republic directed by rigid Christian Scientists would in a very short time be a vast cemetery. There would be no laws enforcing vaccination or prohibiting adulteration in food and drink. Since the purity of milk would be undefended by law, babies would die in their thousands. The deaths of mothers in childbed, already, despite all the arts of the physician and surgeon, a terrible feature of human experience even in the most civilised societies, would be multiplied to an incalculable extent by the substitution of "metaphysical" for surgical obstetrics. The cities would be undrained; the doctors, surgeons, and nurses would be driven out of practice. There would be no provisions for the isolation of infectious diseases. Typhoid, cholera, and small-pox would rage unchecked. A strict execution of Mrs. Eddy's doctrines throughout the world would in a very few years extinguish human life upon this planet.

If Christian Scientists are enabled to sustain existence to-day, it is because they are members of a society which is regulated by principles the opposite of their own. The Christian Scientist, like the inmate of the lunatic asylum, is a social parasite. He can only exist as one of a community which thinks otherwise than he. Living under the shelter of that great body of rules and regulations which every civilised community has built up for the protection of the public health, and profiting by the wise precautions, which are due to the accumulated experience of generations, he can practise a great part of his doctrine with comparative immunity. But if the State were governed on the principle that physical evils are unreal, and therefore not to be feared or provided against by physical means, where would he be? The house in which he lives has been built out of the fear of heat and cold, of rain and snow, and it has been drained as a deliberate material precaution against disease. If he goes out into the street, he finds that the traffic is regulated from fear of accidents. Legislation based upon fear protects him from injurious bacilli in milk, water, and food, shelters him from contact with dangerous infection, and endeavours to counteract the many sources of pollution which arise from the aggregation of large numbers of people in the same place. He would not be able to drink a cup of tea or coffee unless a number of purely physical precautions had been taken for many centuries to prevent shipwreck at sea. The fear of toothache, which prevails very widely among human beings, has provided him with a convenient instrument with which to clean his teeth. The fear of dyspepsia ensures him a supply of tender meat. At every point he finds himself enjoying advantages which flow from the fact that the community of which he is a member has for many centuries regarded illness and accident, not as false beliefs, but as very real evils, to be feared and guarded against by timely precautions.

It does not, however, follow that Christian Science will not continue to attract an increasing number of adherents among those who for one reason or another find the existing forms of Protestant worship unsatisfactory. A religion can rarely afford to practise all that it preaches. Lenin was compelled to concede the principle of private trade, which was in sharp opposition to the Communist philosophy which had given him the mastery of Russia. Mrs. Eddy was obliged to permit vaccination, and recourse in certain cases to surgical aid. In the authorised addresses delivered by the Board of Lecturers we detect a disposition to insist upon the practice of the Christian virtues, upon the evil effects of fear, hatred, jealousy, and depression upon health, and, in vague and general terms, upon the Infinity of God, and the Divinity of man, rather than upon those exorbitant claims of Christian Science to provide the true and only cure for every ailment, which must always be challenged in the court of common sense. By failing to practise all that they preach, and by failing to notice all that they dislike, Christian Scientists may retain their faith and enlarge their numbers. They may find in their Church much that attracts—an excuse for averting their gaze from the ills and sorrows of mankind, a warrant for a high degree of spiritual pride, a form of worship, decent, dignified, relieved by the aid of music, and making no exorbitant demands upon the time of busy people; a theology emancipated from fear and technical mysteries, a sacred book, which is also a talisman against disease. To the vast tribe of female neurasthenics, nowhere so numerous as in the United States, the alleged healing properties of the Christian Science mind-cure make a decisive appeal. But the number of these sectaries who under no circumstances would have recourse to a doctor or a surgeon, who believe vaccination and other forms of preventive medicine to be without value, and are indifferent as to the character of the food which is given to their babies, must be few indeed. It is safe to assume that most men and women who join this Church regard the Christian Science mind-cure, not as the sole, nor even as the most efficacious, but only as the holiest method of curing diseases. However little they may be disposed to give public assent to this hypothesis, their practice will be found to confirm it.

It is significant that the city in which the

new religion is most powerful is not Boston, nor New York, nor London, but Los Angeles, the first health resort in the New World. Amid the credulous, excitable, neurasthenic population which is drawn to this beautiful city by the charm of its climate and the magnet of the films, Christian Science finds countless patients and votaries. In no great American town is the power of education so low, or social direction so weak, or the sense of tradition so negligible. Here every form of quackery and superstition abundantly flourishes. The love of marvels goes with the gambling spirit, and the bright air of Los Angeles tingles with speculation.

To those who believe in the value of literary cultivation, it is a melancholy reflection that a book so devoid of literary or logical merit as *Science and Health* should be accepted as even creditable to its author, and still more amazing that it should be regarded by some persons of education as a work of Divine inspiration. In truth, it belongs to one of those compositions (among which most "best sellers" are to be numbered) which owe much of their popularity to positive defects. Had it been less long, less apocalyptic, less dogmatic, less magniloquent, less repetitive, less paradoxical, and less obscure, it would not have enjoyed so great a vogue among the emotional, half illiterate population who constitute the rank and file of the Christian Science army.

Optimists may be inclined to argue that with the slow advance of education the influence of the Christian Science text-book, and consequently of the Church which has been founded to promote it, must inevitably wane. To these it may be replied that what preserves *Science and Health* is not its style, which is repellent, but its message, which is popular. The new Bible is not valued primarily as literature; it is the dogma which attracts and the dogma has behind it the popular force of a wealthy American corporation.

The vogue of doctrines depends upon their imaginative appeal. What text is at once more familiar and more remote than this: "And God said, Let us make man in our own image, after our own likeness, and let him have dominion over the fish of the sea, and the fowl of the air, and over all the earth, and over every creeping thing that creepeth upon the earth"? But when from this ancient poetry of a vanished world Mrs. Eddy draws the conclusion that man is not made to till the soil, that his birthright is dominion, not subjection, that by mind he can vanquish disease and death and sin, and proceeds to announce that she has herself, by the exercise of powers common to mankind, raised the dead and given sight to the blind, the old text acquired a new and propulsive force. "I could never tell you," writes an earnest American lady, "what a flood of light and liberty filled my heart as I read, what possibilities opened out to me, what promise Christian Science set before me." [1]

Moreover, in estimating the new religion's expectations of life, the brilliant business mechanism constructed by its creator must not be left out of account. The Christian Science corporation is as little likely to founder as the Standard Oil Trust. It commands vast material resources; it directs influential newspapers; it possesses the monopoly of the sale

---
[1] L. L. Coulson, *West London Observer,* Friday, March 14th, 1928.

and distribution of the Church literature; it appoints and dismisses the lecturers and readers. The vested interests of the new religion, considerable in England, are vast in the United States, where many people now regard it as likely to furnish in future years the only serious competitor to the Roman Catholic religion. To dislocate so imposing a concentration of material power will not be easy, for a trust which comes into being to meet a particular demand finds its account in sustaining it. The Christian Science corporation has patented a cure for all ills, and advertises its patent by a continuous exhibition of miracles. No corporation, no trust, no Church, has gone down into the market of the common mind with wares more attractive or more profusely commended. Few commercial companies, pushing a remedy, pure or adulterated, are more lavishly provided with funds. So long as business is business, the corporation in Boston which governs these affairs will not relax its hold.

The Christian Science Church objects on principle to the "numbering of the people,"

THE CHURCH

and declines to publish statistics. We know the names, addresses, and telephone numbers of the registered practitioners, we are supplied with lists of the churches and societies (2,386 in June 1929) dedicated to the observance of the new religion. We know that 3,649 lectures were delivered throughout the world last year, with a total estimated attendance of 2,900,926. These important and illuminating details are communicated to the public in the pages of the *Christian Science Journal,* which is the monthly official organ of the Mother Church in Boston, or in the columns of the *Monitor;* but we have no statistics, we have no official estimate of the total membership of the Christian Science Church. It may be a few hundred thousand.[1] It may exceed a million. Whatever the number may have been the day before yesterday, it is likely to be greater the day after to-morrow, for we learn that a new church is opened every four days.

The absence of numerical statistics may in part be attributed to the fact that the Christian Science Church is not, despite its desire to be

---

[1] Mr. Hendrick (*McClure's Magazine,* 1912) thinks that the membership may have then been between 150,000 and 200,000.

so, a closed Church. It is possible to be a Christian Scientist without severing connection with other forms of religious communion. Mrs. Eddy's *Church Manual* may be searched in vain for a baptismal, marriage, or burial service. If these rites are required of a Church, they must be procured of some other Church. Accordingly, there are Christian Scientists of every degree of thoroughness, some regarding this new religion as a primary and exclusive faith, others regarding it as supplementary, and combining it in differing proportions with older forms of practice and belief. The flaming core of undivided enthusiasm is surrounded by a wide penumbra, shading off by imperceptible degrees into the darkness of unbelief.

Christian Science is an American fabric. In the United States, in Canada, in England, in South Africa, Australia, New Zealand, wherever Anglo-Saxon influence is strong or predominant, the cult attracts adherents, and even enthusiasts. In Germany, doubtless owing to the strong German element in the United States, it has made some advance, for there are five Christian Science churches in Berlin, and

THE CHURCH

thirty other German towns in which the new religion claims a church or a society; but outside the Anglo-Saxon or Teutonic zone the doctrines of the prophetess make little headway. In France, Italy, and Austria, Christian Science is barely discernible. In Spain it is non-existent. In Russia it appears to have one centre only. The Rouman emigrants to Toronto or New York have not yet succeeded in sowing the seed of *Science and Health* among the peoples of the Homeland. Save for two churches in Buenos Ayres, it would appear that Latin South America is, as yet, unaffected.

This is not surprising. The Latin mind is not drawn to a philosopher who first denies the existence of the body and then writes a long book to show how it may be cured, who affirms the unreality of pain but permits recourse to the dentist and anæsthetist to relieve it, and who in one and the same breath instructs us to believe in the Atonement and the unreality of sin. But, apart from the fundamental inconsistencies of Mrs. Eddy's doctrine, there is another barrier hardly less strong which opposes itself to the spread of

Christian Science doctrine beyond the pale of the English-speaking races. *Science and Health* must be read in English. It is true that a German translation, with the English original on the other side of the page, has now been permitted by the corporation, possibly out of deference to Count von Moltke, late Chief of the German General Staff, in whom the Church had obtained its most eminent foreign adherent. The Germans, then, may read Mrs. Eddy in a German dress. The violent vagueness of an ill-organised volume is not wholly incompatible with their natural temperament; but the Latin peoples are otherwise constituted. For them, order, lucidity, exactitude are the first requisites of acceptable writing. In these qualities *Science and Health* is deficient.

It has, then, yet to be proved that Christian Science can make conquests in a Latin country. An Italian city like Florence, which is much frequented by American visitors, will have its little group of lady healers, just as English doctors are to be found at Cannes or Nice, but how many Italians will exchange their gracious Madonna for the grim, capable figure of the American Puritan, who set her face against wine and the use of tobacco, denied the reality of matter, and ended life as a dollar millionaire? In the Protestant atmosphere of the British Empire the chances for the Church are far more favourable. Canada has already fifty-five, and England a hundred and sixty-five, centres of activity. In London there are thirteen, in Manchester five, in Toronto four churches. In the number of its Christian Science practitioners (251) London already eclipses Boston.

This last fact is more significant, since it is the practitioner who brings in the recruit. If the church fabrics indicate the opulence of the past, the healers measure the harvests of the future. "Healing is better than teaching" is one of the wise headings in the *Church Manual*. To teach a metaphysic so paradoxical, so confused and contradictory, so paralysing to common sense, as Mrs. Eddy's philosophy is an enterprise upon which few can embark with any sense of buoyancy or confidence; healing is by comparison an easy matter, and, wherever it meets with success, the most effective form of suasion. The large number of healers in the British capital is therefore the best indication of future progress.

It is a religion for the rich, the eupeptic, the vivacious, this religion which proclaims as unreal and non-existent pain and sickness, fatigue and death, and has no use for the emotion of pity, the fairest flower in the garden of the soul, which the spectacle of human suffering is wont to produce in sensitive natures. It is a religion which brings heart to the hearty, "good cheer" to the cheerful; but what can it say to the dying pauper in the slums which he will not regard as an affront to the lessons of a lifetime? It will tell him that his pain is an error, his illness an error, his poverty an error, his impending death an error. It will tell him that he is suffering from the delusions of a mortal mind, that all that he has regarded as real—his body, his experience, his sufferings—is, in effect, a dream and a delusion, and that the only reality is that which seems to him most distant and fantasmal. To the downcast and the outcast such a philosophy is a cruel mockery. They know instinctively that it is false.

bility of Man pales before the blaze of this misleading and characteristic passage.[1]

The point upon which the Church feels most sensitive to criticism is not the efficacy of its healing virtues, but its claim to Christianity. The evidence of healing, however defective in quality, is now sufficient in amount to impress the mass of the faithful, and is constantly receiving additions. The powers claimed for humanity by Mrs. Eddy are now being exercised by a large number of zealous women, and by a smaller number of zealous men, in every Protestant country in the world. These powers are believed, in an appreciable number of cases, to have been helpful. The Christian Scientist has, therefore, always a reply to the critic who contends that the healers do not heal. He can point to undoubted cures, and to the fact that, in the opinion of both healer and healed, these cures proceed from the same cause—reception of Christian Science into the mind, and the flight of error before it. But the accusation that Christian Science is not Christian is more formidable.

---

[1] "Practising the Allness of God," by Marie C. Hartman, *Christian Science Journal,* March 1929, p. 645.

The new religion is recruited from Christians, who would be greatly distressed to hear that in embracing Mrs. Eddy they were renouncing Christ. There is no way, then, in which the Church could be more severely injured than by a successful demonstration that it had no right to be regarded as a Christian body. A conviction, widely spread among the faithful, that such a proposition had, in truth, been established, would bring the Church toppling to the ground.

No Christian theologian has ever accepted the view that matter is unreal in the sense in which that phrase is used by Mrs. Eddy, or that the spirit is not immanent in the world of our experience. The metaphysics of Mrs. Eddy are fundamentally inconsistent with all the main positions of Christian theology. They are inconsistent with the doctrine of the Personality of God. They are inconsistent with the doctrine of the Incarnation, and they are inconsistent with the doctrine of the Atonement. The doctrine of "mortal mind," apparently self-created, though unreal, and, despite its non-existence, the seat and scene of all the force over which we had no control, to behave as if it were real, then the strain of the new creed began to make itself felt within the mind. Some would break away and leave the Church; others would reinforce their failing courage by all the stimulants which idealism can supply.[1]

In the crisis of ambiguity and of faith the Christian Scientist finds support in the current literature of his Church. There he will discover a note of optimism so violent and hectic as to suggest the workings, somewhere in the background, of a conscience ill at ease with itself. "We always," writes an eloquent American lady, "have the glorious truth to rely on, the protecting fact to cling to, namely, that man, as God's image, is always whole, perfect, free, and safe. All his needs are met, fully and completely met; he lives in Divine love, is guided by infinite wisdom, is supplied with goodness, health, and understanding. In short, man could not be more perfect than he already is; and he never will be other than perfect." Condorcet's doctrine of the Perfecti

[1] M. C. Sturge, *The Truth and Error of Christian Science.*

A thoughtful writer who has now severed her connection with Christian Science has alluded to the "painful strain" and "unspeakable fatigue" of endeavouring to persevere in the impossible belief prescribed by Mrs. Eddy's metaphysic. "Life," she writes, "under such circumstances becomes almost unbearable." At first the neophyte was intoxicated with the glow of this strange revelation. To reject the existence of the material world, to disbelieve in the reality of the body and bodily pain, to hold that Christian Science could really render death obsolete and banish sin, to believe that the possession of a few simple truths about the oneness and omnipotence of God, if sufficiently widely diffused, would enable the world to dispense with doctors and surgeons, and all the paraphernalia of the medicine chest and the hospital—this was, indeed, the opening of a new heaven on earth. But when the first intoxicating rapture had died down, when the scruples of common sense began to prick, when it became increasingly clear that, however much we affirmed to ourselves the belief that the body was unreal, we were nevertheless compelled, by a evils and errors which afflict humanity, finds no place in the Christian view of the universe.

But fortunately for Christian Science, Mrs. Eddy is not a thinker. Few people have a greater capacity for allowing two contradictory propositions to lie down in the mind side by side, undisturbed and unperceived. Few people wielding so wide an influence have been so little capable of deducing a rigorous chain of consequences from their major premises. The Christian Scientist in doubt about his Christianity has only to turn to the Tenets of the Mother Church, prefixed to the *Church Manual,* to find a sufficiency of help in repelling this assault. Here, in six brief and telling sentences, the Founder has laid down the cardinal articles of the faith:

(1) As adherents of Truth, we take the inspired Word of the Bible as our sufficient Guide to eternal Life.

(2) We acknowledge and adore one supreme and infinite God. We acknowledge His son, one Christ; the Holy Ghost as Divine Comforter; and man in God's image and likeness.

(3) We acknowledge God's forgiveness of Sin in the destruction of Sin, and the spiritual understanding that casts out evil as unreal; but the belief in sin is punished so long as the belief lasts.

(4) We acknowledge Jesus' Atonement as the evidence of Divine, efficacious love, unfolding Man's unity with God through Christ Jesus, the Wayshower; and we acknowledge that man is saved through Christ, through Truth, Life, and Love, as demonstrated by the Galilean prophet in healing the sick, and overcoming sin and death.

(5) We acknowledge that the Crucifixion of Jesus and His resurrection served to uplift faith to understand eternal life, even the allness of soul spirit, and the nothingness of matter.

(6) And we solemnly promise to watch and pray for that mind to be in us which was in Christ Jesus; to do unto others as we would have them do unto us; and to be merciful, just, and pure.

"To pray for that mind to be in us which was in Jesus Christ" is, for most pious professors of the new religion, the operative part of the faith. To be charitable, temperate, just, unselfish, to be raised above vulgar temptations and passions—these are no doubt ideals preached by Mrs. Eddy, and practised by many of her followers, and, in so far as the Church is possessed of such a spirit, it may rightly claim a part in the Christian heritage.

It is on the speculative rather than on the ethical side that the new religion invites the attack of the orthodox Christian communities. "Cease," says the Christian Scientist, "to believe in the reality of your toothache, and the toothache will vanish. Cease to believe in the reality of your sin, and the sin will vanish." But if sin is killed by substitution of a belief in its unreality for a belief in its reality, of what use is the saving power of Christ? The Bible, in which we are invited to find "a sufficient guide to the eternal life," gives no countenance to the idea that sin is unreal. Its teaching is just the opposite. That the Christian virtues may be well and helpfully employed in certain forms of mental healing is a proposition which would now find wide acceptance with distinguished medical practitioners, and it is this application of the Christian spirit to the task of healing which constitutes the real strength of the Christian Science Movement. Unfortunately, the valuable part of Mrs. Eddy's discovery is associated with a grotesque and extravagant metaphysic, and with a wholesale repudiation, as ignorant as it is arrogant, of all the medical and surgical experience of the world. Yet such are the frailties of human nature that the historian of religions will hesitate to affirm that the violent absurdity of this faith has not been an important element in its success. If Mrs. Eddy had contented herself with saying that Christianly minded women in many cases could help the sick by directing their minds to Christian truths, and by urging them to make light of their physical sufferings, would there now be over six hundred Christian Science healers practising in Chicago? It was the novelty, the audacity, the paradox of her tenets, which caught the ear, first of the Bostonian, then of the American, and finally of the British public. A little truth mixed with a great deal of extravagance has a knack of travelling far.

The farming homesteads of the American continent have given birth to many strange and fantastic forms of religious experience, and nowhere has the soil been more propitious to the development of new and surprising cults than in New England.

There one wild religious leader after another has risen, stormed his life away in prophecy, and vanished into the darkness whence he came, leaving behind him a following of sectaries which has gradually dwindled or split into fragments, until they too have been absorbed by the gulf of time. Of all these forms and varieties of belief arising out of the strenuous religious consciousness of New England, Christian Science alone maintains its vitality and spreads its influence. Little trace does it bear now of its homely country origin. It is housed in great urban churches, supported by powerful urban newspapers, patronised by the rich and the elegant in every capital. Yet it is a gift from the countryside, perhaps the last gift which that old, unsophisticated, Calvinistic society of New England will make to the religious experience of the world.

No unfair criticism of the worth of a religion is the nature of the spiritual values which it creates or supports. What, judged by this test, are the credentials of Christian Science? What new sources of moral wealth have been unsealed by this religion? What contribution has it made, or is it likely to make, to the art and literature, the science and well-being, of the world? What type of human character does it essay to produce?

Such moral beauty as may be discovered in the writings of the Founder is purely derivative. It comes from Christianity, and from no other source. Of literary and artistic beauty there is none, still less is there discernible that rare and austere passion for intellectual truth which shines in the pages of an Aristotle or a Spinoza. But when it has been conceded that Mrs. Eddy's morality is Christian, an important qualification must be made. Two virtues, high in the Christian scale, are almost entirely foreign to her nature. She is without the grace of humility, and exceedingly deficient in the virtue of compassion. The Christian Science religion fosters, no doubt, a spirit of cheerful courage, which helps its votaries to face the rubs and sorrows of life; that is its peculiar and distinguishing merit. The Puritan in trouble about his health; the neurasthenic; the pleasure-lover, who does not wish to look pain and sorrow in the face; the rare mystic, who can, without violence to the intellectual conscience, live in an atmosphere where spirit is all in all and matter is nothing, may find comfort and support in the teaching of this society. Those, on the other hand, who value beauty, compassion, good sense, and truth must look in another direction.

Nor, save in a restricted sense, does the practice of these tenets nourish the graces of unselfishness. To heal is no doubt to perform a public service, and the virtues of the healer, in so far as she believes in the doctrine of her Church, are those of the medical practitioner. But the general drift of Christian Science teaching appears to be ego-centric. Instead of regarding health as natural, the Christian Scientist holds it to be a state of the spirit only to be won and sustained by mental exercise. So a religion which sets out to banish the fear of illness, in many cases ends by enthroning a valetudinarian anxiety in the citadel of the mind, an anxiety deepened by the belief that the taint of moral and spiritual weakness attaches to every physical pain or discomfort. To be ill in itself is bad enough; to believe that illness is a moral and intellectual disability is worse still; to hold, as did the Founder, that illness or false beliefs may often be caused by the malevolence of an enemy, is worst of all. Here and there, the votary of this creed may pass through life with a careless and easy courage, inspiring others to a like temper of happy gallantry. Such, however, is not the common rule; for whatever useful fruits may be produced by a religion in which health has ousted charity as the main concern, the selfless nature will not be among them.

More than a generation has now passed since the death of the Founder of Christian Science—a period marked, in the religious history of the United States, by an increased effervescence of fantasy, but also by a further development, upon the lines inaugurated by Mrs. Eddy, of solid business trusts framed to supply, upon terms profitable to their promoters, a stock of popular consolations and remedies to the vulgar. Of these organisations, the agency known as Unity, devised in Kansas City by the wit of Charles and Myrtle Fillmore, to cure souls and abolish death by various forms of absent treatment, is now the most conspicuous. Unity, we are informed, issues twelve million publications a year, spends seven thousand tons of ink, consumes three hundred tons of paper, has its United broadcasting station, its Unity Inn ("the larg-

THE CHURCH

est and most beautiful cafeteria in the world") its Unity Farm, and farm buildings heated from its Unity oil wells. "If any man," observes an American writer, "will look at the work which Unity performs, with its seventy-six hundred letters a day, its colossal broadcasting station, its thoroughly capable prayer department, he will understand the methods by which effective religion to-day must function. It is, in brief, a rhapsody in statistics, and therefore the key to modern religious enterprise." [1]

To the student of history there are few subjects more pathetic than the workings of the religious craving in man—his hunger for peace, for ultimate knowledge, for an anodyne against pain and sorrow, for a key to the mysteries. Amid all the transformations of fate, and despite all the rebuffs of experience, the primal craving remains eternal, inextinguishable. But what Protean forms does it not assume, now blunted or sharpened, now ennobled or debased, by the uncertain moral values, the shifting economic stresses, the prevailing human preoccupations of the time! In

[1] C. W. Ferguson, *The Confusion of Tongues,* p. 222.

the keen bustling atmosphere of North America the meditative and mystical creeds of the ancient East undergo a transvaluation. Energy, initiative, good sense, are prized above the quiet and fugitive graces of the soul. The active virtues rise, the contemplative and cloistered virtues descend in the scale. For the Christian Scientist, a brilliant pioneer of drugless healing, spurning the mummeries of Oriental medicine and winning from his infallible cures an everlasting renown, replaces the suffering figure on the Cross.

AUTHORITIES

PRIMARY

MARY BAKER GLOVER EDDY, *Science and Health*, first edition, 1875.
MARY BAKER GLOVER EDDY, *Miscellaneous Writings*, 1897.
MARY BAKER GLOVER EDDY, *Introspection and Retrospection*, 1891.
MARY BAKER GLOVER EDDY, *Manual of the Mother Church*, 1895.
The Christian Science Journal, 1883ff.
The Christian Science Monitor, 1908ff.
H. W. DRESSER, *The Quimby Manuscripts*, 1921.

SECONDARY

BRAID, JAMES, *The Power of Mind over Body*, 1846.
BROWN, CHARLIE REYNOLDS, *Faith and Health*, 1924.
BROWN, WILLIAM, *Psychology and Psychotheraphy*, 1921.
BROWN, WILLIAM, *Suggestion and Mental Analysis*, 1922.
CARPENTER, W. B., *Principles of Mental Physiology*, 1874.
DICKEY, ADAM, *Memories of Mary Baker Eddy*, 1927.
DRESSER, A. G., *The Philosophy of P. P. Quimby*, 1895.
DRESSER, H. W., *Health and the Inner Life*, 1906.
DRESSER, H. W., *A History of the New Thought Movement*, 1920.

DRESSER, H. W., *Methods and Problems of Spiritual Healing,* 1899.
EVANS, W. F., *The Divine Law of Love,* 1885.
FERGUSON, CHARLES W., *The Confusion of Tongues,* 1929.
FIELDING, ALICE, *Faith-Healing.*
FOREL, A., *Hypnotism (English translation),* 1906.
JANET, PIERRE, *Les Médications Psychologiques,* 1919.
JAMES, WILLIAM, *The Varieties of Religious Experience,* 1902.
McClure's Magazine, September 1912.
MILMINE, GEORGINE, *The Life of Mary Baker G. Eddy,* 1909.
MARTIN, PRINCE, *The Psychological Principles and Field of Psychotherapy,* 1911.
MACCRACKEN, *Mary Baker Eddy and her Book, "Science and Health,"* 1925.
MÜNSTERBERG, *Psychotherapy,* 1909.
PAGET, STEPHEN, *The Truth and Works of Christian Science,* 1909.
POWELL, LYMAN P., *Christian Science, the Faith and its Founder,* 1917.
PULLAN, L., *Mrs. Eddy's Christian Science,* 1928.
RAMSAY, E. M., *Christian Science and its Discoverer,* 1924.
STRACHEY, RAY, *Religious Fanaticisms,* 1929.
STETSON, AUGUSTA E., *Reminiscences, Sermons, and Correspondence,* 1913.
STETSON, AUGUSTA E., *Vital Issues in Christian Science,* 1914.
STURGE, M. C., *The Truth and Error of Christian Science,* 1903.
TUCKEY, C. LLOYD, *Psychotherapeutics,* 1889.
TWAIN, MARK, *Christian Science,* 1907.
WILBUR, SYBIL, *The Life of Mary Baker Eddy,* 1908.

AUTHORITIES

Of the Secondary Authorities, Miss Milmine's admirable biography ranks first in authority. Miss Wilbur's work, though characterised by careful research, is uncritically enthusiastic. The recollections of Adam Dickey are of the greatest value for the concluding years of Mrs. Eddy's life.

As an introduction to the general history and literature of mind-healing, I am principally indebted to Pierre Janet's masterly book.